DATE DUE

PRACTICAL DEVOTIONS FOR TODAY'S BUSY WOMEN

STILL MOMENTS

COMPILED BY
MARY BECKWITH

Regal Books

A Division of GL Publications
Ventura, California, U.S.A.

Published by Regal Books
A Division of GL Publications
Ventura, California 93006
Printed in U.S.A.

Library of Congress Cataloging-in-Publication Data

Still moments.

1. Women—Prayer-books and devotions—English. I. Beckwith, Mary,
1945-
BV4844.S75   1989   242'.643   88-36415
ISBN 0-8307-1325-5

2 3 4 5 6 7 8 9 10 / 91 90 89

Rights for publishing this book in other languages are contracted by Gospel
Literature International (GLINT) foundation. GLINT also provides technical
help for the adaptation, translation, and publishing of Bible study resources
and books in scores of languages worldwide. For further information, contact
GLINT, Post Office Box 488, Rosemead, California, 91770, U.S.A., or the
publisher.

Contents

Introduction   15

An Invitation to Our Readers   17

Devotions

Rejoicing in His Love   19
Cynthia Ann Wachner

Thank You for Our Family   21
Gloria Gaither

Reading Letters   23
Beryl Henne

Harvest of Love   25
Josephine Smith

Poured-in Protection   27
Edith Schaeffer

Raise Up a Child   29
Daisy Hepburn

A Special Gift of Love   31
Marla J. Hill

A Prayer for Peace and Perspective   33
Elaine Stedman

How, Lord?   35
Judy Hyndman

Reflections of His Light   37
Carolyn Johnson

Tongue-tied 39
Beverly Hamilton

In the Center of His Will 41
Sharon K. Johnson

Let the Baby Do It! 43
Mary Beckwith

Blues Medicine 45
Shirley Joiner

We Got Us a Commitment 47
Cheryll Kelly

Healing Hearts and Broken Wings 49
Joan Bay Klope

Love in the Shadows of Life 51
Karen Burton Mains

Bite of Truth 53
Sherri Turner Martinelli

Just the Way I Am 55
Jeanie Maxwell

What Wrinkles? 57
Zoe B. Metzger

Just Too Busy 59
Beverly Hamilton

While the Dew Is Still on the Roses 61
Kathi Mills

Let's Go Fishin' 64
Glenda Palmer

Freeing Power! 66
Marge Rearick

My Spiritual Journal 68
Elaine Wright Colvin

All Right, Christopher! 70
Marian Carney

The Real Meaning of Trust   72
Hilda J. Born

Mother No Longer Sings Solos   74
Marlene Bagnull

Gracias, Señor   76
Marlene Askland

A Laugh and a Lesson   78
Niki Anderson

Cracks in the Sidewalk   80
Lynn Abbott

Come Away with Me!   82
Nellie C. Savicki

Joys "R" Us   84
Dorothy Segovia

Our Special Vacation   86
Ingrid Shelton

The Silent Garden   88
Elona Peters Siemsen

Having a Hard Day?   90
Pat Sikora

Letting God Love Me   92
Lou Ann Smith

Into Africa!   94
Andrea Stephens

A Fork in the Road   96
Susan F. Titus

Apron Strings   98
Doris Toppen

A Touch of Love   100
Patti Townley-Covert

Songs of Deliverance   102
Stephanie Vernon

The Case of the Missing Sheets 104
Mary Hamilton West

A Colony of Caring 106
Arvella Schuller

The Brass Apple 108
Jean Westlake

Insignificantly Significant 110
Georgalyn Wilkinson

Stepping Stones of Faith 112
Paula Meiners Yingst

It's No Secret! 114
Mary Beckwith

Blessing in Disguise 116
Kay Stewart

Hawaii, Here I Come! 118
Paula Hartman

Grilled Cheese and Parking Lots 120
Laurie Wardwell

Guard Your Heart 122
Neva B. True

What Shall I Wear? 124
Doris Greig

Prayer Patterns 127
Geraldine Nicholas

Old Charlie Stalled Again 129
Ellen Weber

Star Struck 131
Margaret Brownley

In God's Care 133
Annette Parrish

Flying High 136
Barbara Hyatt

My Hiding Place   138
Berit Kjos

Time to Dry Their Tears   140
Dawn Dulaine

The Right Foundation   142
Jessica C. Errico

Love that Won't Let Go   145
Darlene Sybert Andree

Labor Till the Harvest   147
Debbie Kalmbach

Safe in the Savior's Hand   149
Anna Hayford

In His Time   151
Linda Montoya

He Keeps His Promises!   153
Zoe B. Metzger

Child of the King   155
Rhonda McGarrah

I'm Parched, Lord   157
Gay Lewis

He Never Sleeps   159
Alice C. Peter

God, Where Are You?   161
Anna Hayford

A Choir Robe and a Gag?   163
Martha Bolton

Seeing Jesus   166
Berit Kjos

The Maternity Dress   168
Darlene Hoffa

Going the Distance   170
Marla J. Hill

Blossoms in His Eyes   172
Eileen Hegel

You're a What?   174
Sheryl Haystead

Treasured Memories   176
Shirley Dobson

Love, God   178
Margaret Brownley

God's Plans—Our Possibilities   181
Debbie Kalmbach

Homework   183
Marilou Flinkman

His Heart of Love   185
Lucille Moses

My Special Little Closet   187
Anne Ortlund

Soup till Jesus Comes   189
Marge Rearick

Water-walkers   192
Dorothy Segovia

Hidden Treasures   194
Josephine Smith

Three Strikes—You're Safe!   196
Paula Michelsen

Lord, He Doesn't Know You!   199
Kathleen Parsa

For All Mankind   201
Cheryll Kelly

My Treasures   203
Eloise Busha

The Magenta Colored Blouse   205
Mary Frances Froese

Never Late Again 207
Nancy Graeme Detjen

Treasures to Be Found! 209
Louise B. Wyly

And the Little Children Shall Lead Me 211
Mary Harris

Wrestling Alligators 213
April Hamelink

Hurting—Who Me? 215
Gay Lewis

A Stranger in the Tub 218
Marlene Askland

The Best Time of Life 220
Joy P. Gage

Hearing with God's Ears 223
Doris Greig

Take Your Foot Off the Brake! 225
Paula Meiners Yingst

Kurokujin 227
Georgalyn Wilkinson

Panic in the Fog 229
Mary Hamilton West

Facing Death with a Smile 231
Stephanie Vernon

God's Gentle Reminder 233
Barbara Lockwood

Connecting the Dots 235
Lou Ann Smith

Bagels and Swiss Cheese 237
Paula Michelsen

Alone or Alive? 239
Cynthia Buckingham

Unemployed? Oh, No! 241
Marlene Bagnull

Miracles Do Happen 243
Diane Reichick

Unbridled Praise 245
Joan Bay Klope

You Belong to the Family 247
Daisy Hepburn

Please, Stop the Noise! 249
Andrea Stephens

Adequate to Comfort? 251
Joy P. Gage

The Mud Puddles of Life 253
Marilou Flinkman

Baby Talk 255
Kathleen Parsa

Entries from a Real Mother's Journal 257
Mary Harris

Fast Food and Living Bread 259
Niki Anderson

Don't Forget the Butterflies, Ruthie 261
Wilma Giesser

Postscript 285
Meet Our Contributors 265

Poems

How Bright My Path 20
Eloise Busha

Hymn 32
Judith L. Roth

And I? 42
Geraldine Nicholas

Divine Appointments 46
Elaine Wright Colvin

God Is the One 56
Diantha Ain

Hosanna! 58
Kathi Mills

The Ideal Mother 63
Elaine Wright Colvin

Resurrection Life 65
Kathi Mills

At a Son's Baptism 85
Mary Harris

The Prize 126
Marilyn Hochheiser

Cloud Array 135
Maria Metlova-Kearns

A Fresh New Day 144
Shirley Mitchel

This Day 165
Gloria Gaither

Lovest Thou Me? 180
Geraldine Nicholas

More Christlike 191
Elaine Wright Colvin

Let His Light So Shine 222
Diantha Ain

Ordained Praise 263
Annette Parrish

Introduction

No one knows better than the busy Christian woman the value of a still, calm moment in the special presence of God. We know that He is with us even in the midst of lively children underfoot, untimely interruptions at work and taxi shuttles to soccer practice. But we know also the unique serenity of a moment spent reflecting on His Word and seeking Him in prayer. We share the psalmist's conviction that

He leadeth me beside the still waters;
     He restoreth my soul (Ps. 23:2-3, *KJV*).

The still moments that follow minister in another unique way. Here you can have a cup of coffee, as it were, and an intimate conversation with the authors. These perceptive friends, many of whom you already know from their previous writings, offer also a cup of blessing, inviting you to experience with them the recreative powers of the still waters that restore the soul.

—The Editors

An Invitation to Our Readers

No matter where you are in life, no matter what your station, we believe you'll find yourself within the pages of this book.

Though our circumstances vary, we're not so different, you and I. We all experience joy, we all undergo sorrow, and at times we all meet with fear. The causes for our feelings may be unique to each of us, yet we're bound by the common denominator of our need to express ourselves and then to be comforted.

But we tend to live frantic lives these days. We're busy people—sometimes too busy to reach out to others for help, to give of ourselves to them, and even to reach upward to God.

We need to come closer to the One who is always there when we need Him, the Comforter who knows our need before we even know it ourselves, the One who wants us to come to Him and be comforted. Drawing near to Him enables us, in turn, to reach out to those around us. That's what this book is all about.

As you read and enjoy the real-life stories about women like yourself, our prayer is that you will gain a new and better understanding of how God is at work in the lives of people today, how He loves us like no other and how He communicates that love.

Spend a moment each day with us, won't you? It's an investment that will last a lifetime.

MARY BECKWITH
On behalf of the contributors

Rejoicing in His Love

CYNTHIA ANN WACHNER

To whom then will ye liken me, or shall I be equal? saith the Holy One. Isaiah 40:25, *KJV*

The wedding march sounded, and I stood to watch the radiant bride meet her beloved at the altar. As I turned, the groom's expression caught my eye. Love, joy and desire for her brightened his face as he beheld her in a brilliant white gown. He saw only her perfection and beauty. Truly, he delighted in her.

As she approached him he began to sing, rejoicing in her beauty. His song expressed steadfast love and his desire to provide her every need and protect her from all harm.

It made me think of Jesus, our Bridegroom. As He joyfully sings His love song, He feeds and strengthens us with His Word and we soar like the eagles. He quenches our thirst with living water and our weariness vanishes. He clothes us with a gown of righteousness so we will not faint in His presence. He decorates it with the jewels of His character and the fine gold thread of our faith.

Lord, thank you for choosing me as your bride, the one in whom you delight. Help me hear your love song as you joyfully provide all I need to meet you clothed in your holiness at the altar. Amen.

How Bright My Path
ELOISE BUSHA

How bright my path; how beautiful,
How clear and light the way,
Since Jesus leads and Jesus guides
My steps
From day to day.

How bright my path; how marvelous
It is to know that I
Am safe from fear and safe from harm
Because
My Lord is nigh.

How bright my path; how glorious
To trust in God above,
To know my Lord who died for me
Now lives
And reigns with love.

Thank You for Our Family

GLORIA GAITHER

Surely I have a delightful inheritance.
Psalm 16:6, NIV

Because we so appreciate our own heritages, Bill and I have chosen to live near both our families. We feel there is great value for our children in knowing their roots that give them a sense of perspective and continuity. In a society as mobile as the one we all live in, Bill and I feel very blessed that we've been able to offer our children a close relationship with their extended family and close friendships with their young cousins and aging relatives.

Living close to our extended family has not always been problem free, but we feel the benefits far outweigh any problems. Good or bad, family is family and life is life. We feel children need a realistic view of the influences that have come together to make up the sum total of what they are.

Now that Bill and I, Suzanne, Amy and Benjy have come to be a family ourselves, we draw from the rich heritage we have been given. Daily we work upon this base to build the kind of family we believe God wants us to be. Together we are learning to care more, love more unselfishly, and reach into our communities with compassion.

We know that each of us is still a "kid under construction," and, as children of God, we must help one another become what God wants each to be. Some days it is Amy who helps me to grow; other days Bill lifts Suzanne. At times, Benjy is a great teacher for us all. Together we are growing in the soil of our home, fed and nourished by the nutrients of our shared pasts, from the seeds God has planted in us.

Father, thank you for family members who make up our heritages and influence who we are today. But more important, thank you for the inheritance we have obtained through your Son Jesus Christ. Amen.

Reading Letters

BERYL HENNE

And after I go and prepare a place for you, I will come back and take you to myself, so that you will be where I am. John 14:3, TEV

Eagerly I went to the mailbox—again. *Why was the mail so late today?* Impatiently I searched up and down the street to see if I could see the mailman coming. He was nowhere to be seen.

I went back to the kitchen, but couldn't settle down to get anything done. Then I thought I heard the lid of my mailbox squeak. I rushed down the stairs and opened the door. Sure enough! There was a letter from my husband!

I read that letter about five times that afternoon. It was so good to imagine him talking to me. He was in the primitive country of Irian Jaya—on the other side of the world. To make a phone call was terribly expensive and just about impossible to do. So we had to be content with letters.

This letter made so much difference in my day. I was at peace and felt loved. It was so good to know that he was fine and the work was progressing nicely. His work was nearing completion and he would be back home again soon.

As I put the letter down, my eyes fell on my Bible. I had bought it a year ago and it still looked new. It seemed as if I could hear God saying, "My child, I have written some letters to you as well, but you have not read them so eagerly. I want to talk to you, too. I want to assure you that I love you. I want to make a difference in your day.

"It won't be long now until I come back. And when I do, I want to find you unashamed and ready to return with me, so that where I am, there you may be also. I want you to rest in me and not let your heart become troubled. Enjoy my peace, child."

Dear Father, please help me to be faithful in reading your letters and obeying your directions. Thank you for your love and your peace. I want to trust you more. Amen.

Harvest of Love

JOSEPHINE SMITH

A man reaps what he sows. The one who sows to please his sinful nature, from that nature will reap destruction; the one who sows to please the Spirit, from the Spirit will reap eternal life. Galatians 6:7,8, *NIV*

My VW couldn't hold another person. I had taken several widows to church and returned to pick up some children. A family of six made a car load. One Sunday morning, a little girl stood by and watched as the children climbed aboard. She looked so lonely standing there.

Even though the car was full, I asked if she wanted to go to church with us. She said she would ask her mother if she could go next week. She did go next week, and every Sunday for some time.

That was many years ago. I'm now in my golden years; old age has taken its toll. Life is lonely; two of my children have preceded me in death. I am fearful of the future without daughters to care for me. Old age can be a time of fear and frustration, even with the Lord's presence. To occupy my time, I have become a member of the prayer chain at church. I can do this from my rocking chair.

One day, I received a call to pray for a woman in need. In turn, I phoned her to ask if she'd like to come to my house for prayer. When I answered the door, she threw her arms around me and began to cry. Through her tears, she told me she was the little girl I had taken to church years before. We prayed, and God met her need.

She comes to see me often now. She drives me to church, runs errands for me and cooks little "goodies" to cheer me up. She has become such a blessing!

Harvest time comes to all of us. We really do reap what we sow. If we plant the seeds of hate, greed, envy and strife, we can expect to reap a harvest of the same. Years ago, I planted a seed in the heart of a small girl, and now I am reaping a harvest of love.

Lord, help me to sow good seeds so I can reap a bountiful harvest. Amen.

Poured-in Protection

EDITH SCHAEFFER

Whosoever drinketh of the water that I shall give him shall never thirst; but the water that I shall give him shall be in him a well of water springing up into everlasting life.
John 4:14, *KJV*

I craned my neck to get a better view of the building as the car slowly turned to go up the hill. The angles were terrific as they soared skyward in beautiful dark brown symmetry. *The Steel Triangle—what a fantastic building, fitting into the three rivers and the rest of Pittsburgh and enhancing rather than dominating it,* I thought. "What a lovely brown that steel is—my favorite shade," I remarked. Our friend, who knew well the details of what made up this United States Steel Building, began to tell us some of what could not be seen by merely looking at the outside of the structure.

"See the columns? They rise to a height of over eight hundred feet, and there are eighteen of them. Each column is made up of hollow box sections containing a total of about four hundred thousand gallons of water plus antifreeze." He went on to say that the water was to maintain the strength of the building during any possible outbreak of fire. Without the water, the columns would lose their strength, buckle and collapse.

Poured-in protection! Observable beauty, strength and purpose were easy to see in looking at this especially fine modern building. But a *hidden protection* was poured in to stay—ready for a sudden attack of fire from any side. What a titanic illustration of the marvel of the "water" with which God has promised to fill those who are a part of His "building"—His people.

Water! Life-protecting water is to be poured in and will flow out of the ones who believe on Jesus. The Holy Spirit is to be given, after Jesus is glorified, to *everyone* who becomes a Christian. Each Christian is then promised to be given the water of the Spirit—and in addition to refreshing us, the Holy Spirit is to be a protection to us in times of special "heat of fire." Ephesians 6:16 speaks of our quenching the fiery darts of the evil one by using the "shield of faith." But as I looked at those silent brown columns filled with water, I felt a special comfort in knowing that the Holy Spirit was also filling each of us as a protection against those fiery darts. Satan's fiery darts come from unexpected angles, but the water of the Spirit is there. We have His cooling system as we feel the heat of the attack.

Thank you, Father, for the living water of your Holy Spirit. Thank you that it is ever present to give us much needed refreshment and protection. Amen.

Adapted from the book *A Way of Seeing* by Edith Schaeffer, copyright 1977 by Edith Schaeffer. Used by permission of Fleming H. Revell Company.

Raise Up a Child

DAISY HEPBURN

You must teach them to your children and talk about them when you are at home or out for a walk; at bedtime and the first thing in the morning. Deuteronomy 6:7,*TLB*

My grandmother gave me this Bible," Lisa told our Bible class. "She was a simple lady, without much formal education, but with a love for the Lord and her family. One of the concerns of her heart was her feeling of inadequacy to raise up her children, all seven of them, and to love and serve the Lord."

When Lisa's grandmother asked the Lord for an idea on how to be a greater influence on her children, it was as if the Lord directed her to her Bible. "Yes!" Grandmother mused, "This is what I will do; I will read this precious book through for each one of my children!"

29

So her grandmother did just that—making notes, underlining special verses, personalizing it for each of her children. When she finished reading seven Bibles through, she went to work on her grandchildren. "Here is the Bible my grandmother read for me," Lisa shared.

I, too, feel inadequate at times as a mother. A year ago, I read through a Bible for my son. What a joy to give it to him for his January birthday—all marked up and personalized for him. Perhaps he will never read that particular Bible through to see all the underlined verses, and yes, the arrows to verses he really needs to pay more attention to, I think with a smile, but what it has done for me has been worth it all.

Another grandma I know has set aside a page in her prayer notebook for each of her 13 grandchildren. There she has their own handprint. As she prays for each one, each day, she places her hand on that child's handprint, and asks the Lord to make her a link in the spiritual life and growth of those precious to her—and to Him!

Deuteronomy 6:7 reminds us to teach our children, pray for them and train them up to love and serve Him. How we need the Creator's creativity to make it happen in the dailiness of our lives!

Dear Lord, make me a link in a child's life to you today. In so doing, may I find joy in obeying your Word. Amen.

A Special Gift of Love

MARLA J. HILL

And do good, and lend, expecting nothing in return; and your reward will be great.
Luke 6:35, *RSV*

I remember a very special friend whom I will see again one day in heaven. She taught me many valuable lessons; the most valuable was that of learning to give whatever you have to give.

When my husband and I were in our early years of marriage, with three small children and very little money, Paulene brought a beautiful bouquet of roses from her garden.

She gave the roses, not to me, but to my husband with this sweet note. "I know how much you love your wife and want to share that love in special ways. These roses are for you to give to her."

What a special and precious gift of love from my

husband—and from my friend. Paulene wanted no credit from me; it was only later that I learned of the note. She unselfishly allowed my husband the pleasure of giving the roses to me.

Our heavenly Father blesses us with special gifts of love daily. Yet how often do we scurry around in our active lives, too busy to notice his special gifts, and far too busy to stop and give a few special gifts of love to others?

Dear Father, show me some way that I can share your love today in some special way, asking nothing in return. Amen.

Hymn
JUDITH L. ROTH

come slide down into the deep wet grass
    and watch the slugs slither
    rising from the ground like new shoots of grass
    and sinking again—a note on a zither

lie on your back and watch the bold sky
    just out of reach and stretching up higher
    the swallows are swooping, dizzying your mind
    hawk hanging on wind, a kite on a wire

spring, yawning as she watched the winter pass
    has risen and stretched like the sun
    come slide down into the deep wet grass
    and see what God has done

A Prayer for Peace and Perspective

ELAINE STEDMAN

*Welcome one another, therefore, as Christ
has welcomed you, for the glory of God.*
Romans 15:7, *RSV*

Lord, he's different from me. He's adventurous, I'm cautious. He's confident, I'm diffident (though sometimes we switch these postures). He thinks in broad categories, I read the fine print. In what proportions do these differences come from inherited and environmental factors, from different sets of hormones and genes?

I encounter other differences, too. There are those who are more accomplished, more gifted than I. There are even some who appear more handicapped—or have I measured by the wrong crite-

33

ria? Certainly there are variables in privileges, opportunities and endowments.

But then I'm reminded that you, God, are the only one who can measure our differences and properly assess our worth; and that in your Son we have equal standing, equal opportunity, equal access to acceptance and forgiveness.

Thank you for 2 Corinthians 10:12, which teaches that classing and comparing, measuring one person against another, is foolish and without understanding. I want to learn to value differences and to grow and learn from all kinds of people. I want to be stretched beyond the smallness of my own little world.

Lord, I want to see through your eyes, to appreciate what you approve and forgive what you forgive, both in others and in myself. Make me to be of one heart and one mind with your eternal purposes in others' lives as well as in my own.

Thank you, Lord, for making this prayer possible through your Son. Amen.

How, Lord?

JUDY HYNDMAN

---

*Do not fear, for I am with you; do not be
dismayed, for I am your God. I will strengthen
you and help you.* Isaiah 41:10, *NIV*

I looked out the window and said, "Oh,
no! It's starting to rain!" The path from the front door
to the car looked slick. Anxiety gripped me as I
thought of everything I had planned to do.

As usual, I'd overcommitted myself. I had to get
my daughter to her piano lessons, take freshly baked
muffins to a new neighbor, had to . . . had to . . . And
now with no baby-sitter to watch my toddler, I'd have
even more to carry to the car. There'd be muddy feet,
not to mention possible dangerous road conditions.

Once, a one-way ticket, light backpack, loose
agenda and a "cure thyself" philosophy were all I
needed. Now, several years later, as a wife and
mother, my independence and strength had been
ripped away by a virus, leaving me partially paralyzed.

I remember the dread of unanswered questions: How could I clean a two-story house, be a helpmate for my husband, care for our three-year-old daughter? How, Lord? Fear loomed as I grudgingly went through the motions of recovery.

"Here are your crutches, Mommy." I turned from the window to see little Sean, proudly but awkwardly heaving the twin metal supports toward my grasp.

"Let's go," I said, tossing a diaper bag over one shoulder, grasping the car keys with my teeth and tucking a bag full of recyclable newspapers into my crutch handle. "Come on, Sean."

"Here, Mom, I'll take your arm." Gwyneth, now 10, came alongside, clutching her piano books and keeping an eye on her brother. She confidently supported me along the slippery sidewalk and inside the car.

"My truck!" yelled Sean.

"Oh, could you bring Dad's library books from upstairs, too?" I called out as Gwyneth ran back inside.

"Ready." Gwyneth swung breathlessly into the passenger seat.

"Scary," Sean said as the downpour began.

Yes, it is scary sometimes, not knowing how we will manage unpredictable situations, having to depend on family, friends and even strangers for help. I started the car, feeling my anxious fears roll away, joyful, acknowledging God's intervention every step of the way.

Thank you, Lord, for fulfilling your promise of strength and help in the smallest and largest of life's crises. Amen.

Reflections of His Light

CAROLYN JOHNSON

When Moses came down from Mount Sinai with the two tablets of the Testimony in his hands, he was not aware that his face was radiant because he had spoken with the Lord.
Exodus 34:29, *NIV*

Driving north from Santa Barbara along the coastal highway, I watched the last bright sliver of sun disappear into the Pacific. My class had run overtime, and I'd stopped for gas, so it was later than I'd planned when I finally headed home.

Too soon grey twilight turned to moonless night, and I crept along, searching the darkness for familiar landmarks. This part of Highway 101 was lovely by day, with the ocean on one side and the mountains on the other, but I didn't like driving it at night. My fingers tightened on the steering wheel as I strained to see where the edge of the road met the shoulder. *No use.* I would have to concentrate on as much of the pavement straight ahead as I could see.

I breathed a prayer. "Lord, please keep me on the road."

As I rounded a curve, my headlights shone on an even row of tiny lights down the middle of the highway. *Like little sentinels!* I thought. *All I have to do is follow them home.*

Those wonderful little reflectors on our nation's highways make me think of the guides God provides for me in my Christian walk. Like the reflectors on the road, my fellow believers and I have no light source of our own. But like Moses, those who turn their hearts toward the Giver of all light reflect His glory, shining along life's pathway. How many times I have reached out to my Christian sister or brother for guidance when I have felt lost or for courage when afraid.

As the highway engineers designed the reflectors for our safety and comfort in driving, our Lord provides us for one another as we travel the paths He has laid before us.

Thank you, Lord, for those who reflect your glory and light the darkness as I travel through life. Amen.

Tongue-tied

BEVERLY HAMILTON

But as for you, speak the things which are fitting for sound doctrine. Titus 2:1,*NASB*

Five o'clock at last; I slipped the dust cover over my typewriter. As I did, Sharon, the secretary who sat at the desk next to mine, lingered around my work area. It was obvious by the way she picked up a pen and put it down again that something was on her mind.

With a smile, I sighed, "Long day, wasn't it?"

"How does God speak to you?" Sharon blurted out.

"Through Scripture and prayers," I answered after a brief hesitation. "He ... He ... sometimes ... " My mind went blank.

Before I had a chance to say another word, Sharon grabbed her purse and was out the door, barely taking time to toss a, "Good night ... thanks," over her shoulder.

It never failed. Every time Sharon asked me about God or salvation, I was only able to answer her specific question, and then couldn't think of another thing to say.

I'd been trying to lead Sharon to the Lord for several months and even though I'd brought her to church and introduced her to my friends, I felt I was failing her—and God. And even though I believed God can turn everything to good, I wondered how He could use my silence to His advantage.

One morning several days later, Sharon came running over to me. Her sparkling eyes told me something wonderful had happened.

"I accepted the Lord last night," she said, as she reached over and grabbed my hand. She explained how one of her new friends at church had prayed with her. Smiling, she continued. "Thanks for not preaching to me when I asked questions. Everyone else tried to tell me too much at one time, and I became confused. You simply answered my questions, and told me what I needed to know at the time."

I smiled to myself when Sharon went back to her own desk. God's ways are so mysterious and powerful. He can even use silence to His advantage.

Father, guide my words when I tell others about you, that I may speak the things which are fitting. Amen.

In the Center of His Will

SHARON K. JOHNSON

*I will instruct you and teach you in the way
you should go; I will counsel you and watch
over you.* Psalm 32:8,*NIV*

While helping with a youth camp
recently, I spent my free time walking the bluff over-
looking Puget Sound. I needed to spend time alone
with God to seek His will for my life. There were so
many demands on my time and energy, I felt overwhelmed and fragmented.

"Lord," I asked, "what is it you want me to be
doing now? How do you want me to spend my time?"
I asked Him to direct my life in the months ahead and
to teach me to do His will.

Engrossed in prayer, I walked farther than I had
intended. A brisk wind blew across the water and a
sudden downpour drenched me. I hurried through
the wind-whipped rain the mile back to camp.

Soaked, I longed to change into dry clothes. As I neared the camp, the rain stopped and an enormous rainbow filled the sky. Above it was another rainbow! A dazzling double rainbow encircled the retreat center. I walked across the field to get a better view of this phenomenon.

With the setting sun at my back, I watched the brilliant colors in two perfect arches, God's symbol of His promise to man. Awestruck, I was amazed to see my long shadow perfectly centered beneath the rainbows. It was as if God were saying, "My child, as long as you walk closely with me you will be in the center of my will." And what a glorious place to be!

Dear Lord Jesus, thank you for being faithful. Please help me to walk closely with you so I will always be in the center of your will. There's no place I'd rather be. Amen.

And I?
GERALDINE NICHOLAS

Only a homely,
    helpless,
    bulging,
    earthbound
    caterpillar,
monotonously crawling along
    day after day.

How could it know
    what God intended?

Let the Baby Do It!

MARY BECKWITH

The steps of a good man are ordered by the Lord, and He delights in his way. Though he fall, he shall not be utterly cast down; for the Lord upholds him with His hand.
Psalm 37:23,24,*NKJV*

She was only two: my darling little Miss. Her godmother, Sandy, and I had taken her to a nearby restaurant for lunch. Laura was a delight to take, never a rowdy child, and generally always well-behaved. She was just a little independent, at times.

Sandy and I had a good time getting caught up on all the news of our families and friend, while Laura busied herself with crayons and the paper place mat.

Before too long, the waitress delivered our meals, and as I reached over to cut her food, Laura yelled at the top of her voice. "Let the baby do it!" I looked around. All eyes were looking in our direction. I didn't know whether to ignore her bold statement or scold her for making a scene. Actually, I did neither. Embarrassed, I just laughed—along with everyone else in the restaurant. Looking back, it's fun to recall times like those with the children.

I wonder, though, how my heavenly Father reacts when I shout, "Let the baby do it!" Oh, I don't use those exact words, but I, too, have a streak of independence. I like to run ahead of His timing, striking out in this direction or that, trying to accomplish what I believe is important in life. And in the process, I often stumble, make mistakes and cause myself—and sometimes others—embarrassment.

I'm so grateful for the love of a heavenly Father who knows all about my frailties, flaws and stubborn streaks. His Word says that He is intimately acquainted with all my ways; even before there is a word on my tongue, behold, He knows it all (see Ps. 139:3,4). Yet He loves me with an unconditional love. He loves me enough to have given His Son for me. That certainly doesn't excuse my sometimes rebellious behavior. But it does confirm that no matter how many times I fail, and no matter what anyone else might think of me, my Creator is never ashamed of His little girl.

Thank you, Father, that even when I run ahead and want to do things my way, you make provision for me, because of your unconditional love. Amen.

Blues Medicine

SHIRLEY JOINER

The Lord is good unto them that wait
for him, to the soul that seeketh him.
Lamentations 3:25,*KJV*

Last week I hit bottom. I needed reassurance and encouragement. My husband was watching the Tyson-Spinks boxing match. Dear hubby is not just a boxing fan, he is a boxing fanatic! It was a brief match. Tyson knocked out Spinks in just 91 seconds. However, by the time the commentators dissected every blow, I knew Dennis would be engrossed for an hour. But I needed someone immediately!

The blues swept over me. My only sister within 1,500 miles and her newlywed husband were transferred to Prince George last month. The appointment with the gynecologist nagged at my mind. Decorating

45

and furnishing the new house seemed an overwhelming task. I was tired. There were plenty of reasons to feel sorry for myself. What a temptation. But I refused.

I knew exactly what medicine would cure the blues; a double dose of God's Word. So, that's what I took. The medicine worked wonders! I'd recommend it.

Within half an hour a transformation occurred. None of the circumstances changed. I changed. The resentment melted away and was replaced with contentment. Peace wiped out worry. The loneliness left and longing for fellowship was filled by precious communion with God.

Lord, I'm so grateful you're always here when I need someone. Thank you for being a friend closer than a sister, or brother or husband. Amen.

Divine Appointments
ELAINE WRIGHT COLVIN

God, you're leading me.
With confidence, I face my
day.
Each duty and interruption
are appointments
you've sent my way.

We Got Us a Commitment

CHERYLL KELLY

*He that overcometh shall inherit all things; and
I will be his God, and he shall be my son.*
Revelation 21:7, *KJV*

I sat next to Fred on a night flight across
the Canadian prairies. After listening to the many
adventures of a man 30 years in the business of
catering to northern mining and oil exploration
camps, I asked Fred what he considered to have been
the wisest investment in life.

"My wife!" came the triumphant reply, as a radiant
grin transformed the weather-beaten face into a much
younger looking Fred. Tina, his wife of 25 years, was
the pride of this man's life. She was the one thing that
had remained constant in a life full of uncertainties
and rugged dangers.

And then a shadow of confusion erased Fred's

47

smile. "There's just one thing I can't figure out," he said. "Kids today. They get married and as soon as some tempest or another comes along, they separate. Not Tina and me. We got us a commitment!"

Commitment. A word at once wonderful and fearful. As Fred lapsed into silence, I pondered how often my own commitment to God had been as nebulous as that of the modern generation's toward marriage. Repeatedly, some trial or test of life has caused me to beat a hasty retreat from my commitment to serve Him. In fact, at that very moment I was living in separation from His love because of bitterness over last-minute flight arrangements that had inconvenienced me. I prayed for forgiveness.

Then, reaching over, I gave Fred's arm a squeeze.

"Thanks, Fred," I said, smiling at his bewilderment. "And thank Tina for me, too. I just renewed me a commitment!"

Dear God, I love you. Help me to daily, and without failing, keep the commitment I have made to you. Amen.

Healing Hearts and Broken Wings

JOAN BAY KLOPE

There is a time for everything, and a season for every activity under heaven . . . a time to kill and a time to heal. Ecclesiastes 3:1,3, *NIV*

J ust picture this," I said to my husband as we surveyed our new backyard. "All of those beautiful rose bushes you've given me for my birthdays would go great over there. And we finally have enough room to have a playhouse for Megan. Now I don't expect anything fancy, but wouldn't it be great to place a small hot tub right here at the end of the grass? Seems to me everyone's needs and wants will be satisfied, and we won't be overextending our budget!" I was sure my suggestions were quite good and felt rather smug as I waited for Matt's response.

One look at his face and my heart sank. He told me then that a local veterinarian, who had been rehabilitating hawks and owls for the last 16 years, was turning his attention to other aspects of his profession. "If someone doesn't volunteer to help rehabilitate these birds, local wildlife authorities will be forced to put down even those who have an excellent chance of survival."

That was months ago. Our backyard now has a nice lawn. But large bird cages loom in those places I had envisioned a playhouse and hot tub. Because of my bighearted biologist husband, I have witnessed the healing of many of God's most beautiful creatures. I've also experienced amazing encounters with total strangers who've entered our home, tenderly carrying an array of boxes and blankets housing sick and injured adoptees. Conversations never stay on the birds alone, and I praise God that we've had the opportunity to offer healing words to bird lovers sometimes in great need of encouragement and praise themselves.

The Lord has chosen this situation in my life to show me, repeatedly, that the wisdom of Scripture can be applied continually to our individual situations.

Father, thank you for showing me that there really is a time for everything, and that by killing off the trivial you produce significant healing. Amen.

Love in the Shadows of Life

KAREN BURTON MAINS

*Come, you who are blessed by my Father;
take your inheritance. . . . For I was hungry
and you gave me something to eat, I was
thirsty and you gave me something to drink.*
Matthew 25:34,35, *NIV*

One afternoon, while pounding five-foot iron stakes with a 20-pound mallet in 92-degree heat, in order to anchor the tender fruit trees with rubber hoses against the bending west wind, I noticed I was unusually tired. *It has been a long year,* I thought, then hurried to finish a chapter in a book I was writing. I napped instead and woke feeling feverish. A blood test later revealed I had developed a case of mononucleosis, which lasts for six weeks—if you're lucky. To bed again. I had endured work-stoppage that fall with grace. The illness of my father had tested my faith in the indomitable goodness of the Lord's will. I had looked on my mother's pain with hope for ease. The petty aggravation of broken things—equipment and bodies, had raised a slight spirit of anger; but this, this was the last straw, and my spirit the camel's back. Days were spent on that

51

pillow, head weighing a ton, fever stopping and starting, as I fought despairing whys. I felt like a little
child who had been spanked again and again for some
unknown error. I was willing to change my unruly
behavior but I didn't know what I was doing wrong.

One afternoon Mother came with food. The last
thing she needed was to care for me. "Do you have
this awful feeling that someone somewhere doesn't
like us?" I ventured timidly, afraid to reveal my
stricken feelings.

"No," she replied softly. "I have a feeling that
Someone somewhere knows we won't be the people
He wants us to be without pain. Don't ask where
God's love is. This is His shadow side. It is here in
these bad things." Laying her hands on me, she
prayed for healing. My chastened soul found comfort
and the wounds began to mend.

It is wonderful to find a natural mother who can
give spiritual grace in the midst of her own trials. Yet,
I discovered I was also part of a larger inheritance.
For one year I was dependent on my joint-heirs in the
Kingdom, on my "extended family" of God. They
have turned to me hands of mercy and aid and helps.

This is the larger part of my rich and goodly inheritance, this fellowship of suffering and delight, this
place of belonging in a homeless world.

*Thank you, Lord, for my family, both natural and
"extended." And thank you that you are there at all
times, even when I doubt. Amen.*

Adapted from *Open Heart Open Home.* © 1976. *Open Heart Open Home*
by Karen Burton Mains. Used with permission from David C. Cook Publishing Company.

Bite of Truth

SHERRI TURNER MARTINELLI

If any of you lacks wisdom, he should ask God,
who gives generously to all without finding
fault, and it will be given to him.
James 1:5,*NIV*

Owww! Scott bit me!" whined my five-year-old daughter, Cambria, as she and her two-year-old brother romped on the living room floor. I had just warned my active son Scott there would be consequences if biting occurred.

I promptly carried him to his crib, verbally reprimanded him and reinforced that I loved him but would not allow biting. I asked him to tell his sister he was sorry, and through deep, sobbing gasps he uttered a weak, "Sorry, Bri."

My wide-eyed daughter, who had been strangely silent, watched; her chin started to quiver. She stood tiptoe on the stool next to his crib, gave him a big hug and then softly answered, "I forgive you, Scott."

Cambria had always been empathetic and sensitive to her brother, but her extreme concern and attentiveness to his discipline today made me curious. I asked her to come sit with me on the couch. She nuzzled close and we hugged each other tightly. Trying to understand the roller-coaster emotions of a wise-beyond-her-years five-year-old, I encouraged her to share her feelings.

"I'm just sad that Scott's crying."

Quickly and silently, I prayed for wisdom, then gently asked, "Honey, did Scott bite you or did he almost bite you?" She burst out crying with tears of relief and remorse, "He almost bit me."

We had had many talks about telling the truth and the often unexpected repercussions of "just a little lie." Cambria now understood that her brother had gotten in trouble because she had told a lie. We talked about Jesus and how He taught the importance of telling the truth.

"I'm sorry, Mommy," she said, as tears rolled down her cheeks.

"I forgive you, but Scott is the one who needs to hear your apology."

Soon, we heard him sing out, "Done sleepin' now, Mommy."

Cambria ran to his room. "I'm sorry, Scott. You didn't bite me. I told a lie. Will you forgive me?"

"'S okay, Bri," he said in his usual carefree, I-love-you-no-matter-what voice. Another precious moment was forever imprinted on my heart.

Thank you, Lord, for giving me the wisdom to ask the right question and for letting the consequences of my daughter's actions be her best discipline and teacher. Amen.

Just the Way I Am

JEANIE MAXWELL

I can do all things through Christ which strengtheneth me. Philippians 4:13, *KJV*

Mama, if you eat that fudge sundae you'll be a fat woman!" I'll never forget my young daughter saying this loud enough for the entire restaurant to hear. I immediately experienced "hot flashes"!

Everyone around us that day was either smiling or laughing and our waitress almost dropped her entire tray full of food on the floor. Children can say the most unusual things, can't they!

Weight control is a major factor in many of our lives, almost on a continual basis. We're dissatisfied with our looks, whether it's too many pounds or not enough pounds.

I'm so thankful God loves me just the way I am. It doesn't matter if I'm tall or short, large or small. Sure, I'm convicted to get back to my proper weight. But, even though my weight changes, God's love for me is always the same.

Dear Lord, thank you that you love me just the way I am. Live through me in every area of my life. And thank you for your help and strength in these days of so many temptations. In Jesus' name. Amen.

God Is the One
DIANTHA AIN

Who designed the rainbow?
The earth? The sky? Each tree?
Who conceived such wonders,
Such bold creativity?
Do you doubt that the One
Who made us all
Is the only One who could do it?
I have no doubt;
God is the One.
Quite simply,
That's all there is to it.

What Wrinkles?

ZOE B. METZGER

*I will be merciful to them in their wrongdoings,
and I will remember their sins no more.*
Hebrews 8:12, *TLB*

Little Zoe, our granddaughter, was coming home with us for overnight. Buckled between us in the front seat of the car, she looked up through the windshield at a sky studded with stars.

"I wonder how God keeps the stars up there," she said. "Do you think He uses white glue?"

Grandpa chuckled, and I gave Zoe a squeeze. "I don't know how He does it, Honey, but I do know you are a precious baby."

"I'm not a baby," she corrected me. "I'm four. I'm getting old."

"Oh, no!" I replied. "I'm the one who's getting old."

"Grammy, you're not old." She reached up to touch my face. "You don't have any wrinkles!"

Now, I've left 60 behind and I do have wrinkles. But Zoe looks at me with love; she doesn't see them.

And that's the wonderful way in which God looks at me—with love. Through the eyes of love, He sees me without blemish, made perfect by the sacrifice of His Son, Jesus. He chose me to be a "bright gem for His crown," and fastens me there, not with white glue, but with His promises.

God loves me, and He loves you. Because of Jesus, He doesn't see our wrinkles!

Father God, no doubt I will add a few more wrinkles to my life today. How wonderful to know you will smooth them all out with your unending love. Let me love you more. Amen.

Hosanna!
KATHI MILLS

All the world is filled
   with His glory
as the mountains resound
   with His splendor,
the seas roar
   with His majesty,
and the rocks cry out
   with His praise.

Just Too Busy

BEVERLY HAMILTON

If I speak with the tongues of men and of
angels, but do not have love, I have become a
noisy gong or a clanging cymbal.
1 Corinthians 13:1, *NASB*

My doorbell rang for the third time that
morning. The urge to ignore it was overpowering.
Instead, I yanked open the door and looked at my
neighbor standing there with a measuring cup in her
hand.

"Can I borrow a cup of sugar?" she asked.

With a forced smile I took her cup, stomped off to
my kitchen and clanked the cup down on the
counter. Mounds of sorted laundry in front of the
washer, breakfast dishes in the sink, the vacuum
cleaner in the middle of the living room floor all filled
me with an urgency to get my housework done. And
to top it off, I had a meeting at the church in just a
short time.

But I knew my neighbor was lonely and the borrowed sugar was only an excuse to visit. When I turned to hand her the sugar, I saw her looking at the pictures and plaques on my kitchen wall. Her eyes flitted from "Friends are always welcome," which hung over my door, to "Love one another," above my sink.

In an instant I saw my behavior through her eyes. When had I become so busy that I allowed plaques and pictures to tell about God's love, instead of showing it myself? What was the use of doing church work if I ignored the lonely friends and neighbors around me?

I pulled out a chair for my neighbor and put the tea kettle on the stove. Then I asked her, "What's the rush?"

Lord God, thank you for opportunities to show your love to others. I never want to be too busy to care about those people you put in my life. Amen.

While the
Dew Is Still
on the Roses

KATHI MILLS

*There was a garden, which He and His
disciples entered.* John 18:1, *NKJV*

I first came to the garden some years ago
when my youngest son, Chris, was only five. We had
just moved from the slow, rural pace of farm life in
Washington to the fast-lane living of Southern California; I had gone from being a full-time mother to a
full-time member of the work force; and Chris was
starting school for the first time.

One evening, as I sat relaxing after work, Chris
became very frustrated with his toys. In a fit of anger,
he threw them across the room and began to cry.

Before I could react, I felt impressed to be still and *listen* to my child.

"Stupid toys!" he sobbed. "Stupid toys and stupid house, and not even any trees! I don't want to play anymore!"

I knew the toys were not the reason for his frustration and rebellion. But how could I help him?

Then he looked up at me and said, "If we just had a little garden or something! We can't even have gardens or pets or anything in this dumb apartment!"

"Chris," I exclaimed, "that's it! We'll have a garden! A wonderful garden, full of flowers and trees and animals and . . . "

I smiled. "Close your eyes and you'll see."

I took his hand. "Here we go, out the door and around to the garage. See that little fence behind the driveway? It has a gate. Why don't you open it?"

I paused, then whispered, "Oh, Chris, isn't it beautiful?" I sniffed the air. "Can you smell the roses?"

I heard him sniffing. "I can! Let's pick some!"

We toured the garden, admiring the flowers and trees, laughing with a delight at the chipmunks and squirrels, feeling the sun and wind, listening to the birds and frogs.

"Chris," I said finally, "I think someone else is in our garden."

"Someone else?" he asked. Then, with the faith and innocence of his age, he cried, "I know who it is! It's Jesus!"

The three of us have had some great times in that garden over the years. We've dangled our feet in the cool water, squished mud between our toes and picked strawberries for breakfast. We have even done

62

some serious problem-solving there. Jesus is a wonderful listener. I guess that's because He knows how important gardens are. It was in a garden He found the strength to say, "Not my will, but thine . . . . "

Thank you, Lord, for the quiet place we can find in you. Amen.

The Ideal Mother
ELAINE WRIGHT COLVIN

A lot of love—a lot of grace
A cheery smile to brighten the place.

A lot of patience and faith in me
When I spill my milk or skin my knee.

A little discipline when I need to be good
To help me to learn to live like I should.

A mom that puts God first place in the home
So that from His Word I'll never roam.

There are some things my mother should be
If she's to make a good daughter of me.

Let's Go Fishin'

GLENDA PALMER

*Always be prepared to give an answer to
everyone who asks you to give the reason for
the hope that you have.* 1 Peter 3:15, *NIV*

As I stood in one of those long checkout
lines in the grocery store, I realized, uncomfortably,
that the young man in front of me kept glancing my
way.

"That's a nice necklace," he finally commented.

"Thank you," I answered with a smile, instinctively looking down at the gold chain and fish around
my neck.

"What is that? A fish?" he asked.

"Yes, it's an early Christian symbol."

"What does it mean?" he persisted.

"It's just a symbol a lot of Christians wear," I
answered casually.

The cashier waited on him next. As he picked up his grocery sack and was leaving, he asked me one more question, "Why did you miss an opportunity to share the reason for the hope within you?"

At first, I was irritated. He had tricked me. He was already a Christian. But, what if he hadn't been?

As I drove home, I was reminded of the lady in the beauty shop who had asked if I were a "Pisces" when she noticed my fish necklace. Maybe, just maybe, I could have given her a glimpse of Christ right then. How many other opportunities have I wasted?

Lord, make me sensitive to people who have open ears and help me to become bold in what you mean to me. Amen.

Resurrection Life
KATHI MILLS

As the glory that is Easter
breaks softly through
    the frozen hearts of winter,
faith blooms triumphant
    like the crocus of spring,
bringing hope and joy to those
    who dwell in darkness
and eternal life to those
    who know the Risen
Christ.

Freeing Power!

MARGE REARICK

For the word of God is living and active.
Hebrews 4:12, *NIV*

I was thinking the other day how easy it is to grow complacent about the freeing power of Scripture in our lives. The Lord often touches my memory and takes me back to experiences—some I'm not proud of—so freeing that I can't doubt the power of God's Word.

At first, heroin was just a hobby for me—a way of escape, a break away from some of the pressures I was facing and some of the scars of emotional pain I experienced as a child.

One day when my "delivery" arrived at my door, it came wrapped in what looked like pages from the Bible. Faceup, as I started to unravel my "fix" that would set me free from life's pain, was a simple phrase, "Jesus wept." Just those two little words were enough to reach down to the bottom of my heart and remind me of Christ's love. It was that little passage of Scripture from John 11:35 that would eventually direct me to the One who loved and cared for me, and who had a message for me, even when I was farthest away from Him.

Remembering experiences like this one renews my enthusiasm to read again and again other messages God has sent my way—messages full of the freeing power of Jesus Christ.

Thank you, Lord, for your Word that frees, challenges and reminds me of how near you really are, even when I'm far away from you. Amen.

My Spiritual Journal

ELAINE WRIGHT COLVIN

Guard my words as your most precious
possession. Write them down, and also keep
them deep within your heart.
Proverbs 7:2,3, *TLB*

Keeping a journal was always a great idea—something I wanted to do "when I had lots of free time," but something I had procrastinated starting. So when the invitation came to speak for the church women's group, I was literally speechless.

"Lord, how do I narrow down a topic sufficiently to share your working in my life?" I cried.

And as so often happens, my eyes fell upon an underlined verse in the open Bible on my lap. "Write down for the record all that I have said to you," came the words from Jeremiah 30:2.

And that's when I knew I had to start faithfully keeping my journal. My journal not only reminds me of God's leading and guidance in my life, but it also attests to God's faithfulness in answering prayer, providing for my needs. It is a constant reminder that He's never failed me yet—and that He won't.

As I faithfully began keeping my journal during the month prior to speaking at the women's meeting, it became a record for me of how I was growing in the Lord, how I relied on His promises in His Word, and how He was daily bringing into my life just what I needed most.

Now, 10 years later, I know I can look back and find the answers to questions like: What was God doing in my life last year? When was the last time He spoke to me personally from His Word? What Scripture passages have become especially significant in my life? What circumstances made them real to me?

Sure, a lot of experiences I figure I will never forget, but I do. An evening spent rereading some of my journal notes is like renewing many warm and wonderful relationships. It helps me apply the scriptural admonition of Psalm 103:2: to "forget not all of God's benefits."

Lord, in my moments of discouragement, lead me back again to my journal so that I might say with the psalmist, that "I shall remember the deeds of the Lord." Amen.

All Right, Christopher!

MARIAN CARNEY

*Call to me and I will answer you and tell you
great and unsearchable things you do not
know.* Jeremiah 33:3, *NIV*

Mom! Mom! Let me show you something! Mom, watch this," Christopher screamed.

My patience was thinning. He had asked me just moments before to watch him practice swimming. Over and over, while I was trying to relax, this little guy was calling for my attention.

"All right, Christopher," I responded. "I'll watch you this time, but after this you play with your sister, and stop calling me so much."

As I settled back in my chair, I wondered if there was anything the matter with this kid. Or, was there something wrong with me? Was I simply being selfish?

Sipping lemonade and reading, his dad lay stretched out on the chaise lounge next to mine. Why wasn't Dad being called every few minutes?

This was supposed to be everyone's time of relaxation around the pool. Why, then, was *my* time being interrupted?

Perhaps this was simply the behavior of a six-year-old boy, I thought. We were rather inexperienced, having had three daughters before our "wet" little Christopher.

Finally, curled up for a little nap, I was reminded of God's love for us. Whenever we call on Him, He's standing ready to listen. There's no situation too big or too small for Him to give His full attention to. I'm so thankful He's on call 24 hours a day, and He never loses His patience!

Thank you, God, that you're interested in everything your children do, and that I can call on you in every situation and for my every need. Amen.

The Real Meaning of Trust

HILDA J. BORN

Trust in the Lord with all your heart and lean not on your own understanding; in all your ways acknowledge him, and he will make your paths straight. Proverbs 3:5,6, *NIV*

To celebrate our twenty-fifth wedding anniversary, we attended the Mennonite World Conference in Wichita, Kansas. At lunch on the first day of the conference, we realized that in our haste to pack we left behind our traveler's checks.

In addition, at lunch, we met Jake and Tina, a couple from our hometown, whom we had rarely seen before. Now, thousands of miles from home in British Columbia, we spent some time together. In conversation we had voiced our annoyance at misplacing our money.

The gathering crowd consisted of about 9,000 people, so we were surprised to see these folks headed toward us on the following day.

"We've talked about it," they said, "and we've decided we will lend you our credit card so you can have a good conference holiday."

We were overwhelmed. We didn't know what to say. These people truly trusted us.

Back in our room we concluded that maybe this was why God allowed us to come to the conference: to teach us what trust really means. We can trust Him to supply and stand by us in everything, even when we are far away.

Dear Father in heaven, help me to trust you more in everything and everywhere, with big things and with small. Amen.

Mother No Longer Sings Solos

MARLENE BAGNULL

For I am convinced that nothing can ever separate us from his love. Death can't, and life can't. Romans 8:38, *TLB*

When I was a little girl, every Thursday night I went to choir practice with my mother. The director allowed me to sit next to Mother and encouraged me to sing along.

I beamed with pride. My mother was the best soloist in the choir! I leaned against her and tried to make my voice sound like hers, but almost always mine squeaked on the high notes she hit so clearly.

Mother held the music and turned the pages. When I got lost, she pointed to the right note. I didn't understand all the words or know how to read the notes, but I have no doubt that my love for music, and for the Lord, was nurtured through those weekly choir rehearsals.

Tonight I picked Mother up at her apartment and took her to choir with me. Her voice is no longer strong. It cracks on the high notes and slides off key. She isn't asked to sing solos anymore.

Mother's hands get tired holding the music. She forgets to turn the pages and loses her place. I ask her if she wants to look on with me. She nods her head yes.

I think about the doctor's prognosis. Mother isn't that old, but she has a dementing illness similar to Alzheimer's. She is not going to get better, and it's only a matter of time—no one knows how long— before she gets worse. As a friend once described it, "Something is eating her brain."

Suddenly my thoughts are interrupted by the words we're singing. I feel God's presence. He reminds me that even though we grow old and weary, He never changes. He never stops loving us. He will always be with us.

I glance at Mother. She may no longer be able to understand the words she's trying to sing, but I know His Spirit is touching hers. He will allow neither death nor life to separate her from His love.

Thank you, Father, for your promises and for the many ways you gently reassure me that you are with me and with my mother. Amen.

Gracias, Señor!

MARLENE ASKLAND

I will delight myself in thy statutes: I will not forget thy word. Psalm 119:16, *KJV*

*Q*uanto?" my short Guatemalan friend asked. He wanted to know how much the Spanish Bibles were.

"Fifteen dollars for this one. Ten for this one," I answered, writing the numerals down.

He reached in his pocket and handed me fifteen dollars for the one he wanted.

"*Gracias, hermana* (sister)."

"Thank Dios," I said, pointing to God.

He fell to his knees and holding the Bible up to God, he looked at us as though he wanted us to pray with him.

My husband and I quickly went to where he was and knelt beside him.

"Gracias, Señor, para mi Biblia," he prayed. *"Gracias!"*

After my husband prayed that God would use the Bible to strengthen him and those he would share it with, our friend laid his hand on my shoulder and in Spanish prayed for me. He then placed his hand on my husband and prayed with him.

We arose from our knees, as tears fell from our eyes. We had truly been touched by the Lord through this humble brother.

"Have you ever seen anyone so grateful for the Word of God?" my husband asked as the man left our house.

Oh, Lord, I want my love for your Word to grow stronger day by day. Help me never to forget your Word—it is my life! Amen.

A Laugh
and a Lesson

NIKI ANDERSON

Be not afraid, only believe. Mark 5:36, *KJV*

Serving as a missionary teacher to high school girls in Kenya, East Africa, brought both laughs and lessons. Bible was a required subject—a missionary's dream opportunity.

Fears ranging from witch doctors to cobras permeated the lives of our young students. Added also to their cultural fears was the dread of malaria, a common illness transmitted by the anopheles mosquito. The unwelcome symptoms included headache, fever, nausea and aching limbs.

Malaria was prevalent in our vicinity. *"Suna,"* translated "mosquito," was the apt name of our mission station. Recurring bouts of malaria ultimately shortened my own missionary term.

In my Bible classes I had emphasized the power of Christ to free us from fears, hoping to strengthen their trust in God. I had striven to imprint upon their hearts the simple words of Christ, "Be not afraid, only believe."

One afternoon I retreated from Kenya's intense heat into our cool mission house to correct Bible tests. The test format was to fill in the blanks. One sentence read: Be not afraid, only _____.

I felt pleased as I reviewed one paper after another with the correct answer. Halfway through the stack of tests, I came across one which read: Be not afraid, only *malaria*! I was instantly humored by the answer, while my red pencil moved quickly to check it incorrect. Yet, I thought, how suitable a response for a malaria plagued people. I realized how truly powerful was this young girl's rendition of the Scripture. Then I asked, Was God speaking to me through this babe? God was my Healer. I needed to view my problem as "only malaria." I had been plagued for months by this sickness; but I too must not fear.

Since that day I have "filled in the blank" with fearless belief for many personal tests. For example:

Be not afraid, only *an earthly loss.*

Be not afraid, only *a financial tight spot.*

Be not afraid, only a *childhood stage.*

Indeed, is there ever a circumstance or plight we need to fear if we will only believe?

Be not afraid, _____.
(fill in your own situation).

Lord, help me keep a divine perspective of my problems by refusing fear and believing your Word. Amen.

Cracks in the Sidewalk

LYNN ABBOTT

*Do not fear, for I am with you; Do not
anxiously look about you, for I am your God.
I will strengthen you, surely I will help you,
surely I will uphold you with My righteous
right hand.* Isaiah 41:10, *NASB*

Don't step on a crack or you'll break
your mother's back." Maybe as a child you followed
this law religiously. I personally was enslaved to it.

I even wondered what terrible things my mother
would suffer if I stepped on two or more cracks. I
knew I had stepped on my allotted first crack. Would
crack number two break my mother's arm? Or would
it simply break her back a second time? Or maybe, I
hypothesized, the second crack would *heal* the first
crack's broken back. My career as a chronic worrier
had thus begun.

Cracks consume the mind. You and I become so
absorbed by them we often fail to see anything else—

good or bad. I probably couldn't tell you much today about the scenic route to Oak Elementary School, but I could describe a few cracks.

Cracks and worry cause trouble. I know. I've been fighting them for years. Friends and family warn against the anxiety addiction. But when worry calls, I crawl back.

When I grew weary of daily worries and found that it sapped the energy I needed for endurance, I began to look for answers. I turned to Solomon, who wrote in Proverbs 12:25, "Anxiety in the heart of a man weighs it down, but a good word makes it glad" (*NASB*).

Solomon recognized that not only does good news relieve worry but so also do good words. It's nice to know God doesn't just leave us with a pious pray-and-forget-it formula. In Philippians 4:8 God tells us to replace anxious thoughts with thoughts of the lovely, pure, true and honorable. It's tough to do, but it works. We won't become heroines overnight, but we will get our eyes off the cracks!

Father, help me to get my eyes off the cracks. Let me trust you and focus on those things that are lovely, pure and of good repute. I know you can handle my fears. Amen.

Come Away with Me!

NELLIE C. SAVICKI

Then Jesus went up on a mountainside and sat down with his disciples. John 6:3, *NIV*

The clear, crisp mountain air—the breath of God—renewed my spirit. I had come with other women of our church for a winter retreat at Lazy F.

The cascading mountain stream proclaimed God's glory. The stream's crescendo, like the Hallelujah Chorus, lifted my emotions. I saw the grandeur of God in the shadows and the rich earth tones and in the herd of elk and deer at the feeding station.

Falls broke through the frozen mountainside— faith bursting forth in praise.

The crystalline flakes enwrapped the earth— God's mantle of love.

There was sharing time and a time of silent meditation. Reflecting on the direction I was going and communing with God enriched me.

The crowds following Jesus left little time for teaching God's way. Jesus gained new strength when He retreated to commune with His Father. "Come apart with me," Jesus urged His disciples. It was in times of solitude that He was best able to teach them.

I need to respond to Jesus' invitation. When I hunger for God's way, I am filled with the bread of life. When I search diligently God's Word, I discover truth. When I reach out in prayer, I am given a cup of living water to quench my thirst.

God's love feast is spread before me, a spiritual feast for all my needs.

Almighty God, I need to come apart from everyday activities and reflect on the meaning of life. Amen.

Joys "R" Us!

DOROTHY SEGOVIA

The joy of the Lord is your strength.
Nehemiah 8:10, *KJV*

In the midst of burn-out, mid-life crisis and hot flashes, my damaged receptors wouldn't receive promises of joy. I had used up all my strength keeping feelings exiled and pretending pain away. Suddenly, a Sunday sermon screamed the joy of the Lord all over me and whispered the truth that feelings follow actions and joy follows rejoicing.

I wondered: *Is a flickering faith a saving faith?* Yes, for God's mercy takes what's burned out in me and fires up the joy of my salvation!

Nehemiah reminds us that even flickering faith is a gift of God's Holy Spirit. We know that our sorrows can turn to joy, our shadows into sunshine and our burn-out into brightness.

Joy is warm and radiant and clamors for expres-

84

sions and experience. God commands us to rejoice so joy will radiate even in circumstances that sap our strength and burn us out.

Let's practice rejoicing regularly in order to experience joy. Let our lips and lives proclaim *Joys "R" Us* to a wounded world.

Thank you, Father, that there is strength in the joy that comes from knowing you! Amen.

At a Son's Baptism
MARY HARRIS

From the moment of your birth
I have risked mortality
to honor an earthly covenant.
Questioning the significance
of my maternal role, I searched
for portent, some sign, a vision,
which had eluded me until now
I behold His glory in your radiance,
reflected in crystalline water,
and measure my eternal worth.

Our Special Vacation

INGRID SHELTON

I am the Lord your God, who teaches you what is best for you, who directs you in the way you should go. Isaiah 48:17, *NIV*

Come with me by yourselves to a quiet place and get some rest," I had read in Mark 6:31 (*NIV*) the evening before our family vacation. How I longed to have a complete rest from the activities connected with our home, especially at the end of this busy summer. Yet we planned to see most of the Oregon coast and do some shopping in Seattle and Portland as well, trying to pack in as much as possible in six short days.

When we arrived at the Oregon coast from our home in British Columbia, we knew there was something wrong with our motor home.

"We'll get you on the road again by tomorrow," the mechanic in Seaside assured us.

"This is an interesting place to spend a day," my

husband remarked as we walked along the beach promenade.

The following day the mechanic was still working on our motor home with little hope of completing the job, since he needed a part from Portland. The prospect of seeing the rest of the Oregon coast grew dimmer as day after day went by.

Disappointment filled our hearts. Why did God permit this to happen, we wondered. Should we have stayed at home? Yet everything had seemed so right to go. When we finally pulled out of the gas station on the sixth day, we knew the Lord had arranged this vacation for us. During the five days in Seaside with no transportation to go anywhere else, we did a lot of walking and resting. How we enjoyed the glorious sunsets, the marshmallow roast at the beach, listening to the endless rhythm of the rolling waves, watching the children's parade in town, the delightful home-cooked meals at the Christian Lighthouse restaurant. And finally we were able to catch up on the mountain of reading we had brought along—just in case.

"This was the best vacation I've ever had," our teenage daughter said on the way home.

I agreed. Psalm 46:10, "Be still, and know that I am God," (*NIV*) had become more precious to me.

What had seemed like a tragedy had turned out to be a blessing. How thankful we are to have a heavenly Father who gave us a truly restful vacation, one we will always treasure.

Thank you, Father, that the changes you bring into our lives always work out for our good if we trust in you. Amen.

The Silent Garden

ELONA PETERS SIEMSEN

How natural it is that I should feel as I do about you, for you have a very special place in my heart. We have shared together the blessings of God. Philippians 1:7, *TLB*

Like a softly faded photograph, she's still in my mind, sitting under her lemon tree. Driving somewhere, we discovered we were in her neighborhood. And there she was, on a chair under her tree.

When we emerged from our car, her puzzled look told me she didn't recognize us. My husband gave his name.

"Oh!" she exclaimed. "How could I forget you!"

We decided to give her some of the food my family had just shared with us—fried chicken, peach cobbler, homemade bread. Her face glowed with gratefulness. "This will last me for several meals!"

Our five-year-old was carefully watching this frail old woman, and I could tell questions were forming. "Do you have a car?" she asked her.

A small darkness crossed her face. "No, and that's my big problem. Getting a ride." She said that not one student from the college comes to see her now. I looked across the street at the students' residence on the corner. Lively sounds drifted over to us. Laughter, shouting, music.

Too soon, we needed to go. We helped Mrs. Johnstone up the steps onto her back porch. She looked at me through the screen door. "We had some good times, didn't we?"

"Yes, we did."

"I always had some pop for you."

"And—beer?"

"Yes!" The old sparkle danced in her eyes. "And beer—root beer! So you remember that!"

At our car, I turned and blew her kisses. She blew some back. For a long moment, I wanted to be a college girl again, sitting on the old parlor rug. I wanted to smell once more the dozen old-house fragrances, and to feel the thousand secret memories that warmed that room. I wanted to hear the stories of her beloved, their courtship, their missionary days. I wanted to be urged on to higher adventure by her exhortations and strong tenderness.

As we pulled away from the curb, I looked back to the lemon tree, the silent garden, the little house so full of yesterdays. Good-bye, dear friend. Stay with God.

Oh, dear Father, help me to ever treasure the dear saints you place in my life. Teach me how to learn from them more deeply, how to serve them better. And please help me never forget to tell them thanks. Amen.

Having a Hard Day?

PAT SIKORA

*Dear friends, since God so loved us, we also
ought to love one another.* 1 John 4:11, *NIV*

Even before breakfast, I knew it was
going to be one of those days. Suffering from a back
injury, I had not slept well. Now I was both
exhausted and in pain. It must have been contagious
because three-year-old Joshua whined and complained about everything. I knew I couldn't deal with
this behavior all day.

"Honey," I said in the most gentle voice I could,
"Mommy is having a hard day. I really need you to
help by being good."

Instead of his usual, cheerful, "OK, Mommy,"
Joshua put his head on the table and cried, "I having
a hard day, too!"

As expected, the day went downhill from there. Each time I corrected Joshua, which seemed to be constantly, he would sob, "Mommy, I told you I having a hard day!" Somehow it didn't matter that I felt the same way.

By the end of the day, I was sure I had been through a very long war—and had lost! Even a nap didn't help either of us.

That night I had to attend a meeting. When I got home, more exhausted than ever, Joshua was still awake. He bounced out of bed and with a big smile, raced over and soothed me with kisses and hugs.

Amazed, I stared at him. "Joshua, you've had such a rough day. Where in the world did you get all those kisses and hugs for Mommy?"

Without hesitation he grinned, "Jesus gave me lots of kisses and hugs, so now I have lots for you."

I often learn theology from my young son, but this lesson topped them all. Jesus Christ has already shown me by His death and resurrection how much I am loved. The Holy Spirit is available to me daily, at a moment's notice, to renew my heart and mind. Yet all too often, I ignore these mighty manifestations of His presence and instead wallow in my feelings.

I've decided that now, when I'm having a hard day, I'll remember that Jesus has already given me His kisses and hugs in His love letter to me—the Holy Bible. When I acknowledge and accept them, I can then share them with others in need.

Lord Jesus, help me remember that you always have all the kisses and hugs I need, even on a hard day. Amen.

Letting God Love Me

LOU ANN SMITH

But God demonstrates his own love for us in this: While we were still sinners, Christ died for us. Romans 5:8, *NIV*

I had dragon breath. My hair was sticking out in 15 different directions. No makeup. Runny nose. And, worst of all, I was wearing my ancient used-to-be-white terry robe with chocolate-stained cuffs.

Just as I curled up on the couch, pulled the morning paper into my lap and took a sip of hot honey and lemon tea, the door knob jiggled. Then it turned.

The children had gone off to school and this wasn't Bible study day. Who could it be? What a surprise it was to see my handsome husband coming through the door, a full day early from a business trip.

"You're so cute," he grinned as he let go of his

suitcase and wrapped his arms around me. "I love you, Honey. It's so good to see you."

He's either blind or he's lying, I thought as I pulled away. Kirby seemed a little offended by my response, but before we were married I promised myself my husband would never see his bride looking ugly. And today I looked ugly!

I've since learned a valuable lesson: We can receive love even when we feel unlovable. It's a choice we make.

Even the Creator of all beauty didn't need to wait for us to be presentable before He showered His love by sending His Son to die on the cross for us.

How often I turn and hide from God when I need His tenderness and attention the most. Sometimes I feel stained, unworthy, spiritually ugly. *He couldn't possibly love me like this*, I think, as I pull away and miss blessings He longs to give.

The eyes of love are tender. Their giving gaze is unconditional.

So today, I've made a choice to allow God—and others—to love me, to believe them when they say they do and to receive all the joy and abundance that comes with that decision.

Lord Jesus, forgive me for the times I thought your love was too shallow to accept all of me. From now on I choose to receive your love and care, and I won't turn away when you tell me you love me. Amen.

Into Africa!

ANDREA STEPHENS

Answer me when I call, O God of my righteousness! Thou hast relieved me in my distress; Be gracious to me and hear my prayer. Psalm 4:1, *NASB*

Lions and elephants and baboons. Oh, my!

The reality of my husband's trip to Africa was finally hitting me. I was panic-stricken with fear, angry with the missions committee for ever suggesting the trip and irate with my husband for accepting the challenge. Besides, the big joke while I was in Bible school was that the worst place God could ever call you to serve was Africa.

Not only did 35 days with six high school students, living with the Maasai tribal people and flying on foreign airplanes sound very threatening; it just seemed like more than I could handle. My husband had already given the majority of "our" time to his job as associate pastor. Now that job was requiring him to go spend over a month in a potentially dangerous situation and he was saying yes. I, of course, was saying no!

I began to ask every trusted friend to pray for Bill's decision, for changed lives in the six kids and to have God confirm in some way—any way—that this escapade to Africa was His will and plan. I secretly and selfishly was praying that God would change Bill's mind or that the trip would fall through. I just didn't want Bill to go.

As our prayers reached the throne room of God, a puzzling thing happened. God didn't change Bill or the plans for the trip. He changed me!

One by one my fears were calmed, my outlook on the trip brightened, and—you'll never guess—I decided to go along.

As I prepared for Africa, I thanked God for answering my sometimes selfish and fear-filled prayers the way He saw fit. After all, Father knows best.

Dear Lord, help me to be more trusting as I step out to do the things you have called me to do. Let me rest in the assurance of your all-knowing wisdom. Amen.

A Fork
in the Road

SUSAN F. TITUS

Show me the path where I should go, O Lord;
point out the right road for me to walk.
Psalm 25:4, *TLB*

I gripped my son's hand tightly as we hiked along the path through towering redwoods. The massive trees shut out most of the sunlight. A light fog made the trail difficult to see.

Suddenly we came to a fork in the road. My son asked, "Which way do we go, Mom?" His eyes conveyed trust. He assumed I knew the direction out of the woods.

I paused for a moment and thought of how often forks in the road of life confront us. Frequently, when met by a fork, I have made split-second decisions that have affected my entire life. How different, I wondered, my experiences might have been had I chosen other paths.

Yet, our decisions need not be made alone. God wants us to consult Him concerning even the smallest decisions in life. Through prayer and reading the Scriptures, we can stay in tune with God's direction for our lives.

I looked down one fork of the trail, which divided the world's tallest living trees. Then I gazed down the other. In the distance I saw a light, which I recognized as the sign on top of the mountain cabin resort where we were staying. With confidence I could say, "This is the right path. Let's go."

Dear Lord, guide me as I come to the many forks in my life's journey. Help me to make the right choices along the way. Amen.

Apron Strings

DORIS TOPPEN

My son, observe the commandment of your father, and do not forsake the teaching of your mother; bind them continually on your heart; tie them around your neck.
Proverbs 6:20,21, *NASB*

Apron strings" need not be negative. They represent a positive bond that holds families and lives together. God binds us to each other and the apron strings of our love provide the nurturing that families long for.

Through wear, wrinkles and smudges, an apron hangs faithfully and protects, just like a mother's love. Whether by a tug from a toddler or teen, mothers sense the needs. She can extend her apron strings, reel them out like a kite and pull back, when necessary, to provide freedom and support to grow.

And because our children learn from our walk with God, parents need His apron strings. When we tug at God, He reaches down to fill the desires of our hearts. As we cling to our eternal God and pass His treasures in His Word to our children, we all find wisdom for freedom and growth.

As I raked the yard last week, I was apron-string thinking. Tears filled my eyes as I looked toward our kitchen. Our daughters used to bargain to cook dinner on raking night to escape the trauma of yard work. They would turn up their music and enjoy a good laugh, as I cranked up the rake in rhythm.

That was so long ago. Oh, to have one of those evenings back!

Then I realized those bonds still abound. In fact, they have multiplied. Just yesterday our oldest daughter and family came to bike. Our youngest and her husband were coming tomorrow night to work on a job resume. Perhaps tonight there would be that cherished call from our oldest son's children— "Grandma, may we spend the night?" And our youngest son sent notes from college.

Celebrate apron strings—not the smothering kind, but those that bind together. Apron strings are the fibers of family life.

Dear God, bind your love in our hearts that we may witness to your teachings and faithfulness. Amen.

A Touch of Love

PATTI TOWNLEY-COVERT

And moved with compassion, He stretched out
His hand, and touched him, and said to him,
"I am willing; be cleansed." Mark 1:41, NASB

I never used to be a toucher. Don't touch me! Don't invade my space! Don't come too close because maybe you won't like what you see in me, or maybe I won't like what I see in you. This was my solid stance on the matter of people getting close enough to touch.

When I was a young woman, Jesus reached out and touched me. Frequently, over the years, He has stretched out His hand in compassion, touching me in unmistakable ways. These touches have been in the form of those who have reached out, because of their love for God, to give me a hug, or take my hand at a time when it was desperately needed.

From years ago, when I was a single mom, I can still remember a man who came up to me at church and gave me a hug. That hug taught me more about Jesus' love than the sermon did that day. I was hurting, alone and had not had anyone reach out to me in a very long time.

Recently, at a conference during a time of prayer, a dear man took my hand and held it solidly in his, showing his care. The very strength of God filled my soul by that simple gesture—the touch of a hand. That touch met me right where I was and strengthened and encouraged me in such a way I couldn't help but recognize the Lord's presence in its action.

Since Jesus has touched me, I want to extend His touch to others. There are so many people who are hurting, alone and afraid; there is no finer demonstration of Jesus' love than for me to take their hand, or give them a hug.

Lord, help me to look past myself to others. Enable me to stretch out my hand and touch someone with your love. Amen.

Songs of Deliverance

STEPHANIE VERNON

*And at midnight Paul and Silas prayed, and
sang praises unto God: and the prisoners
heard them.* Acts 16:25, *KJV*

In 1969 I lived in Bouddhanoth, a small
village in Nepal. Although it was a very religious place
to Tibetans, it lacked Christian witness. I prayed God
would let me fill this need, and He answered. He let
me establish an indigenous New Testament church
there.

We met in my apartment building, the ground
floor of which sheltered cows, buffalo and goats. My
apartment was on the second floor over the stable. In
the congregation were Tibetan lamas, Hindu yogis, a
Brahman priest and Nepali believers. Together, we
sang Christian hymns, each in our own language. We
might have sounded like "Babel," but everyone there
loved and respected the Lord Jesus.

Although I preached in English, the people understood. One amazed lama (Tibetan priest) said in Tibetan, "Teacher, I do not speak English, but I understand you," thanks to the Holy Spirit, the perfect Interpreter.

I prayed for our church and wondered how long it would last, for in the words of a Nepali official, "Christianity in Nepal is number one offense and punishable by imprisonment."

One day following the church service, I was arrested and taken by truck to another village, where I was jailed. I had a cheese sandwich and my purse. That night rats ate the sandwich in my purse. When I stepped outside to the field—my bathroom—two guards with bayonets sprang in front of me. Then they stood guard, one on each side of me.

My cell joined the police inspector's room, with only a bamboo curtain between. One day when the inspector was out, I began to pray and sing loudly: "I am a stranger here, within a foreign land; My home is far away, upon a golden strand; Ambassador to be of realms beyond the sea, I'm here on business for my King."

The inspector returned unexpectedly and heard me singing. He concluded that to sing under such circumstances, I must have gone berserk. I was taken back to Bouddhanoth and released. Once more, a prisoner had praised God in song, and cell doors had sprung open! I remained in Nepal 15 years, preaching and teaching the Bible

Thank you, Lord Jesus, that your power to deliver is the same today as it was in the days of Paul and Silas. Jesus Christ, the same yesterday, today and forever. Amen.

The Case of the Missing Sheets

MARY HAMILTON WEST

She makes coverings for her bed.
Proverbs 31:22, *NIV*

Well, I tried! Maybe I wasn't Supermom making coverings for our beds, but I could put fresh, clean sheets on them each week! What's more, I had taught the kids to do the same.

Now, this week was special. We would be entertaining a popular radio preacher overnight. Never had our home held such a renowned guest. Brand new sheets for his bed were called for, since all ours were as old as our growing family.

But, where were they, the beautiful floral set, still new in their package? I had placed them carefully on the linen shelf to await a big occasion. A frantic search ensued, the children were assembled and questioned. Finally, I burst into tears.

Angrily I scolded the son upon whose bed the new sheets were found. There was not time to launder them now. The same old worn white ones would have to do for our guest. Why, I asked our small son, had he taken the guest sheets for himself?

"But, mother," he sobbed, "they were so pretty, and I never slept on pretty sheets before, so I put them on my bed."

Oh, what remorse filled my heart. How ashamed I was. Did I think the needs of a guest to be more important than those of my children? They were special guests in our home, too; God had sent them to us to nourish and care for. They were our ministry. I might not forget their physical needs, but neither must I fail to minister to their spiritual and emotional needs, as well.

Yes, even with pretty sheets!

P.S.—The guest speaker never minded. He just chuckled and thought his sheets were fine!

Only I had minded.

Please, Lord, forgive me when I try to impress someone. Help me keep my priorities straight, and be attuned and sensitive to my family's feelings, even secret yearnings. Amen.

A Colony of Caring

ARVELLA SCHULLER

*May you be able to feel and understand, as all
God's children should, how long, how wide,
how deep, and how high his love really is.*
Ephesians 3:18, *TLB*

Home is the place where, when you
have to go there, they have to take you in." Through
the years, these words from the beloved poet Robert
Frost have sparked in me an amused and understanding attitude as I have watched the family come home,
one by one—happy or sad, angry or "hyper," fighting
or withdrawn. Anyone who lives in a family knows
the many moods that cross the thresholds of our
homes each day, but because we are a "colony of caring," we open the door, hold out our arms and we
love!

What is a family? To the positive believers it is a
colony of caring, a priceless treasure.

When we care about each other, we show that we care. In our first year of marriage my husband learned that I had a special love for a certain brand of chocolate turtles. One day when he came home from work, he made a special production of presenting me with two such chocolates in a bright paper bag. That was all he could afford. If I remember correctly, they cost fifteen cents each. This little gift-giving ceremony was such a precious moment that it became an instant tradition.

Now, once a year, my husband still presents me with a gift of my favorite brand of chocolate turtles. I eat them oh so sparingly, not so much because of my diet, but because I want to savor the memory of his special gesture of caring, [over] thirty years ago.

When we take a positive look at the family, we discover that the family is a treasure chest of people who are caring deeply for each other—so deeply that they go out of their way to do something beautiful for each other day after day, year after year.

Thank you, Lord, for your marvelous love for me. Help me, in turn, to show that very same love and concern to each member of my family. Amen.

The Brass Apple

JEAN WESTLAKE

He found him in a desert land, and in the waste howling wilderness; he led him about, he instructed him, he kept him as the apple of his eye. Deuteronomy 32:10, *KJV*

I opened the office door and glanced in. The secretary was busy at her desk. There was a wooden table with a lamp placed neatly at its center, two occasional chairs, a file cabinet, and on top of the cabinet a brightly shining small brass apple. When my eyes caught a glimpse of this sparkling fruit, all else seemed insignificant. Off and on during my entire conversation with the secretary, my eyes automatically went to the apple. It was beautiful!

"I don't need a brass apple," I said to myself, "but someday maybe I'll find one in a store and my husband will buy it for me for a special occasion." Well, that didn't happen. And between the Lord and me, each time I saw the beautiful brass apple, I admired it more.

For over a year I had been teaching a singles Sunday School class, and several times had quoted from Deuteronomy 32:10: We "are the apple of His eye." Christmas Sunday rolled around and when I walked into the Sunday School classroom, I saw a neatly wrapped package on my podium.

"Open it, open it," the class said. Excitedly I worked to reach the contents. I became all thumbs, but soon I was able to carefully remove the tissue paper that held a large brass apple. My mouth fell open.

"Oh, no! I can't believe it!" I cried, as I held it up for the whole class to see. Engraved on the front of the apple—which was also a bell—was "Deuteronomy 32:10—from the Joyful Singles."

As tears began to fall, I exclaimed, "God is so good!" and proceeded to tell the class why I was so taken with their gift. We all rejoiced together.

The Lord supplies our needs, and many times gives us our wants. Matthew 6:33 says, "But seek ye first the kingdom of God, and his righteousness; and all these things shall be added unto you" (*KJV*).

Isn't it wonderful to know we are His children. He knows us by name. We are the apple of His eye!

Thank you, Lord, for food, shelter and clothing. And thank you, too, for the many added blessings. Amen.

Insignificantly Significant

GEORGALYN WILKINSON

With all my heart I will praise you. I will give glory to your name forever, for you love me so much! Psalm 86:12,13, *TLB*

My thirty-sixth birthday had been special. David, my wonderful husband, had seen to that. But just 12 days later, I stood by his hospital bed watching him fade into eternity.

Life had been so full. What more could I have wanted than to be missionaries to a desperately needy country like Japan? We were excited with our assignment there. Never could I have dreamed that on a mission trip to Korea David would have encountered physical problems which would in three short days take his life.

I stood beside his bed—numb and totally alone. I didn't know another woman in Korea. My precious daughters, six and eight years old, were at home where loving neighbors reached out to them in my place. They read to them about where their daddy had just gone to live. The girls had never thought so much about heaven before. It was not only exciting, but beautifully inviting—a real place!

The thing I least wanted to do on this trip was to shop—for anything. But I hated to return home with no gift at all for my little girls. On my way out of my hotel to the airport, I passed the gift shop. Not a toy or child's item was in sight. But there was a display of a very inexpensive, but typical, souvenir of Korea—the topaz stone. Quickly, I purchased two tiny necklaces and tucked them into my bag.

Our reunion was tearful, but wonderful. I gave them the insignificant gifts I'd found just before leaving. My eight-year-old burst out, "Mom, have you ever read Revelation?!"

"Well, yes, as a matter of fact, many times."

But before I could say more, she jumped with delight, for there in her hands she actually held a topaz, a piece of the place her daddy was now standing. "It's the ninth layer, Mom!"

I could have given her no greater gift, for a chunk of heaven was hers that day—and would always be. And I would always know that "He doeth all things well."

Lord, remind me often today that you desire to be seen in others' lives, through my unconscious surrender to being completely yours. Remind me that everything that touches my life in some way touches eternity. I love you. Amen.

Stepping Stones of Faith

PAULA MEINERS YINGST

He set my feet on a rock and gave me a firm place to stand. Psalm 40:2, *NIV*

A gently lapping current caressed my ankles as I measured my steps along the shoreline of Lake Almanor in northern California.

Looking into the clear, cold water, I marveled at the seemingly cobbled pathway that wandered perpetually ahead of my tender feet. How deceptive it had proven to be. Beneath the inviting crystal ripples lay small jagged rocks that threatened my balance and made each foothold feel awkward and insecure.

This is similar to my walk through life, I thought. *Each sharp stone is like a daily trial that seems inten-*

tionally positioned to test my faith.

Then I came upon a large flat rock, an oasis in the sea of menacing stones, and hopped onto it. I felt grateful for the reprieve offered by its smooth, solid surface. The cool water continued to lap against my ankles, but didn't seem nearly as powerful now that I was standing firmly on the rock.

"Jesus will never leave you nor forsake you," a reassuring breeze seemed to gently remind me. "He will never expect more from you than He knows you can bear."

The next time hurtful stones of circumstance threaten, I'll try to imagine myself at the edge of the lake, my feet set securely on the Rock.

Lord Jesus, thank you for the inner peace and joy that comes from knowing you. Thank you for being my oasis. Amen.

It's No Secret!

MARY BECKWITH

I am not ashamed of the gospel of Christ: for it is the power of God unto salvation to every one that believeth. Romans 1:16, *KJV*

Knock, knock," I heard coming through the door to my office.

"Oh, hi. Come on in," I replied. "What's up?"

I could tell by the look on her face she had something exciting to share. She pulled a chair up close to my desk.

"It's not for public knowledge," she began, "but I just couldn't wait to tell you and a few others." And with that, she told me her good news. "Can you keep it a secret for a few days?" she finished.

"Sure," I promised.

Apparently, someone couldn't keep my friend's secret, however, for soon the whole office was buzzing with her news.

Funny how "secrets" can sometimes spread like wildfire. The things we shouldn't be sharing we are. And the things we should be sharing, we aren't—like words of love and encouragement. Or our time and resources. Or . . . the gospel of Jesus Christ.

How often I go about my daily business and never bring up the name of Jesus to anyone. How often I'm blessed, yet never share the source of my blessings with others. I have my salvation—a promise of life eternal in the presence of my heavenly Father—yet how often do I extend the salvation invitation to someone else?

I still do the things I shouldn't and don't always do the things I should. But with God's help, I want to commit to stop sharing the secrets of others and start sharing the good news of Jesus Christ!

Father, thank you for your forgiveness when I share information I shouldn't. Give me the boldness, and present the opportunities, to share the greatest news of all. Amen.

Blessing in Disguise

KAY STEWART

*For it is God who works in you both to will
and to do for His good pleasure.*
Philippians 2:13, *NKJV*

A church in a nearby community had
hired me to develop a day-school program for young
children. The room they gave me for an office had
once served as a storage room. Windows on one side
and locked storage cabinets on the other presented a
problem for my own paper storage and filing needs.
The room had barely enough space for my desk, a
chair and one work table. Plus, there stood a long-
silenced, antique Victrola that went halfway up the
wall, right in the corner where a filing cabinet should
stand. It had to go! I wheeled it into the hall and forgot about it.

The next day, it was back in my office. I moved it
out again, and took my complaint to the church secretary.

"I'm afraid you'll have to keep it in your office.

116

There's no other place for it," she smiled apologetically.

"But, why don't we just get rid of it? I'm sure no one uses it."

"Oh, we couldn't do that. Someone donated it to the church and no one remembers who that was. It might hurt someone's feelings."

Back in my office I viewed the offensive piece of furniture. *All right, if it's not going to be moved, I'll use it myself.* Inside the cabinet there were vertical slots for records. *A good size for file folders,* I thought. Then, something caught my attention—a piece of masking tape with writing on it. My heart stopped as I recognized the handwriting. *George C. Alkire.* My husband's grandfather! But how? I knew the family had never attended this church or lived in this community. And Grandpa had been dead for five years. Running back to the office, I told the secretary, "I know who the Victrola belongs to!"

"Who?" she glanced up from her typing.

"Me!"

We later discovered that Grandpa had donated it to the Scout troop of that church when my husband's older brother had belonged, nearly 30 years before.

When I'm on a quest, I tend to bulldoze ahead. Sometimes God places an obstacle repeatedly in my path to get my attention. Often I have found in that obstacle a key to opportunity. And in this case I discovered a true blessing, as well.

Dear God, thank you that you're always ready to give me something special. Help me to approach with reverence even what seems to be an obstacle, for it may be a blessing in disguise. Amen.

Hawaii, Here I Come!

PAULA HARTMAN

Trust in the Lord with all thine heart;
and lean not unto thine own understanding.
Proverbs 3:5, *KJV*

As a travel agent for the past 15 years, the opportunity to travel has been a real blessing. Every now and then an airline company will sponsor a contest to win free tickets. One such contest was held a couple of years ago. By selling certain flights, agents accumulated points that would allow them to travel anywhere the airlines flew. I love Hawaii, so I made that my goal.

After only a couple of months, it seemed I would have enough points for one coach ticket to Hawaii. Boy, was I excited! The last week of the contest I retotaled my points, only to find I was several points short. Confused and disappointed, I went to bed that night and prayed, "God, you know how much I love Hawaii. Please let me go. You know how important this is to me."

It wasn't until the end of the week, as I lay in bed about to pray my usual prayer, that a strange sensation came over me. I felt as if God were telling me to give my little dilemma over to Him. My prayer came out slightly different that night. "Oh, God, I have been so selfish. Please let me give this over to your control. I know now that if it's meant to be, it will be."

The next day at work, I found that the contest had been held over for two more weeks. In those last two weeks, I sold enough flights so that I received not only one *first class* ticket to Hawaii, but two coach tickets to Hawaii and one coach ticket to Boston as well. There were even extra points left over to help a couple of other agents win their trips!

Sometimes I get so caught up in the activities surrounding my life and in what I need to be doing that I forget I have a heavenly Father who knows and cares about my every need and desire. Once in a while, He likes to remind me that He is the source of all my blessings.

Dear God, please help me to trust in you for all things. I know that what's meant to be, you will bring about. And that you'll provide, even more than I could ever imagine! Amen.

Grilled Cheese and Parking Lots

LAURIE WARDWELL

Never let your brotherly love fail, nor refuse to extend your hospitality to strangers— sometimes men have entertained angels unawares. Hebrews 13:1,2, *Phillips*

Grilled cheese and parking lots don't have a lot in common, but to me they're inseparable. When someone mentions hospitality, I think of grilled cheese sandwiches and a parking lot filled with prayers.

Every Sunday night for four months my husband and I got together with another family after church. We just didn't want the time to end. Because none of us had much money, we fell into the habit of grabbing a loaf of bread and some cheese. Then we'd snuggle into their small apartment.

Those were times of great ministry in my life as we shared our struggles and how the Lord was working in our lives. The grilled cheese sandwiches could have been sirloin or cardboard for all we cared. It was the time we spent together that was important.

At another time in our lives, we had spent months with six other couples in a midweek Bible study. It was a time of great personal trials for us. I thank the Lord for a couple who knew my husband and I were troubled over something. Most of those in our group didn't even realize we were hurting. But this couple, who have since become two of our best friends, were sensitive to our needs.

After study one night we stood in the parking lot just talking, when they brought up our troubled demeanor. They gently asked if they could pray about anything for us. As we shared, they helped us to reveal the true problems we faced. Then they asked, "Do you mind if we just take a moment now and bring this before the Lord?" We were deeply touched. It was then we learned there's no better time to bring burdens to the Lord than the very moment the need is shared.

Grilled cheese and parking lot prayers have shaped the way I minister to the needs around me. They've made me more sensitive to the troubles and the small things that in the long run really matter the most.

Thank you, Lord, for friends and the small things in life. May we take hospitality to the needs of those around us. Amen.

Guard
Your Heart

NEVA B. TRUE

*But I am afraid, lest as the serpent deceived
Eve by his craftiness, your minds should be led
astray from the simplicity and purity of
devotion to Christ.* 2 Corinthians 11:3, *NASB*

I stared at the paper fluttering across our
driveway. It didn't resemble the usual throw outs.
Hopping out of the car, I investigated. It looked like a
tiny jelly roll.

As I opened the rolled-up paper, I sensed the gentle probing of God's Spirit: "This is only a message
from man. Are you as eager these days to read God's
message?"

Quickly, I defended myself: "I know that message.
I've read the Bible all my life."

My spirit had been pricked, but curiosity won.
The paper heralded the grand opening of a pizza parlor. I thought about it all afternoon. It whetted my

appetite. I whizzed through my least favorite job—putting groceries away.

That evening my family and I visited the pizza parlor. The food looked yummy, but tasted like lead to me. I knew the Holy Spirit grieved over my flippant answer to His question, "Are you as eager to read God's message these days?"

Pushing down pizza, I silently prayed, "Lord, that was a foolish reply. Knowing facts from the Bible isn't getting to know you. I've missed you this year. I need your love message. I want your counsel."

Once again, joy bubbled inside me. But as we rode home I reflected on what had happened in the busyness of this year. Meaningful times with the Lord had dwindled. Off guard, my hunger and zest dried up. When I most needed spiritual nourishment, the enemy worked to keep me from it. He'd deceived me to think that only great chunks of time counted. Unable to read the Word of God that way, he kept me on guilt trips. Craftily, Satan led my mind astray from the simplicity of loving Jesus and valuing even a few of God's precious words.

As we drove in the driveway, my heart sang. The ever-faithful Holy Spirit had used a wisp of paper to whisper truth to my starving spirit. He took a tiny message, looking like a jelly roll, and pointed me back to the sweetness of my Savior.

Lord, I want to focus on you. Help me to keep on guard so my mind will not be led astray today. Amen.

What Shall I Wear?

DORIS GREIG

*Love, joy, peace, longsuffering, kindness,
goodness, faithfulness, gentleness, self-
control.* Galatians 5:22,23, *NKJV*

It would be a time of rejoicing with our
longtime friends, the parents of the bride. And, as
always, I asked myself before the wedding, What
shall I wear?

I know this is not unique with me, for whenever I
call to invite friends for dinner or to a social event, the
women always ask the same question. In our society
we are so conscious of being properly dressed for an
occasion that our attitudes often get in the way of
actually enjoying the event.

This is not so in other cultures. I remember my
missionary friend from Kenya who suffered culture

shock when she came back to the United States, because of the affluence and the daily choices she now had to make. She told me that in her little village in Kenya the women never owned more than two dresses. One was old and ragged, yet clean. This garment was worn by a woman during the week in which to do all her heavy work. The second dress was a better one. Though often very old, it was worn only to Sunday church services and other special events during the year. I'm sure not one of these dear women asked, What shall I wear?

In fact, many of them would give away one of their dresses to any woman in the village who became a believer in Jesus Christ. Often, the poorest woman had only one dress, so a Christian sister would show her love by giving her the best dress she owned.

"Then what do the ladies who gave their best dress away wear to church?" I asked.

My friend replied, "They gladly wear their ragged, but clean, everyday dresses."

These Christian women put into practice what God tells all of us to do in Galatians 6:10, "Therefore, as we have opportunity, let us do good to all people, especially to those who belong to the family of believers" (*NIV*).

Somehow, as I think about my Christian sisters in Kenya, it doesn't seem quite so important what I wear to the wedding. My outward adornment is not nearly so important as the living Savior I have within me. I want His Spirit to enable me to show forth His love, joy, peace, long-suffering, kindness, goodness, faithfulness, gentleness and self-control to those who will attend the wedding and to all I meet daily. May people not remember the dress I wear, but rather how I allowed Jesus to dress my spiritual life with the fruit of His Spirit.

Today, dear Lord, may people see your life lived out in my words and actions. Adorn me with the beauty of Christ so that others will see Him in me. Amen.

The Prize
MARILYN HOCHHEISER

Looking behind I glimpse
people I love
stumble and fall
in the race we run,
and I stop to help them
back on their feet.

Instead I am trapped
in the commonplace,
the undertow pulling me.
I take a deep breath
and start to run
as if for a prize.

Turning my head
toward Jesus,
I entrust Him
to bring
the other runners
across the finish line.

Prayer Patterns

GERALDINE NICHOLAS

*Delight thyself also in the Lord; and he
shall give thee the desires of thine heart.*
Psalm 37:4, *KJV*

Recently, I've made some disturbing discoveries about my prayer patterns. When I'm feeling low or particularly bogged down with cares or problems, talks with my heavenly Father are long and frequent. Meticulously, I outline all the details of my dilemma, revealing my innermost thoughts and concerns. During the good times, however, when my life is full of happiness and fulfillment, my conversations with God become oddly abbreviated—much shorter and to the point.

It's human nature, I suppose. But I know how much I love it when my own children settle down and talk to me about the insignificant happenings in their lives. I feel so much more a part of their lives then.

It seems, though, that when they're feeling rejected or sad, when things have gone a little sour in their lives, that's when they turn to me for reassurance and help. When they're needing something or are in the midst of some crisis, that's when we have our longest talks. But when things are going well and their lives are busy and happy, our meaningful conversations are much less frequent.

Surely, my heavenly Father would be pleased if I would give Him equal time, sharing pleasant experiences and thoughts when my mind isn't cluttered with the storms and stresses of life.

Just simple things. Insignificant experiences. Scattered observations. Cheerful chatter. So many things I can share!

Thank you, Father, for your presence with me during the good and bad times of my life. May I learn to delight in sharing with you the happy experiences of my life, as well as in asking your help during the sad and difficult periods. Amen.

Old Charlie Stalled Again

ELLEN WEBER

"For My thoughts are not your thoughts, neither are your ways My ways," declares the Lord. Isaiah 55:8, *NASB*

It was raining that morning. And we had left a little late.

"Mom, if I get a late slip, I get a detention," said Tanya, my 14-year-old.

With not one minute to spare—I had a Bible study to lead in a short time—we realized that we had neglected to let Charlie, our old Chevy, warm up.

Tanya and I had had more than one laugh over Old Charlie. But this morning no one laughed.

Charlie protested to the abuse first by grinding to a halt at the first intersection past our house. Then we stalled again when I slowed down to turn the corner.

"Don't worry," I assured my daughter, looking at my watch. "If we nip through the Woolco parking lot, we'll still make it." It might have been a good idea, all right, but the first speed bump struck back, and Old Charlie's motor shut down.

Not that he hadn't pulled a few similar tricks before. One day he spit the fan belt out in two pieces. But today Tanya and I were both depending on a quick trip. I could feel Tanya's panic level rising.

"Somebody might stop," I suggested. But nobody did. Rain pounded on the windows.

Tanya gulped, "Let's just look under the hood."

"Why bother?" I sighed. Neither of us knew anything about cars.

But Tanya insisted, "Maybe it'll be something obvious, like the radiator fell off." We laughed and jumped out in the pouring rain.

Everything looked normal enough to us. "Lord," I prayed, "we really need your help. You know about cars and we don't." We got back into the car, and I turned the ignition. Old Charlie purred like nothing had happened. Once again, we were on our way.

Lord, I don't understand your thoughts and your ways. Truly they are higher than mine. I'm just so glad I can call out to you when I get in over my head. I love you, Lord. Amen.

Star Struck

MARGARET BROWNLEY

When they saw the star, they rejoiced with
exceeding great joy. Matthew 2:10, *KJV*

When I was in second grade, I landed a
leading role in the Christmas pageant. I was ecstatic.

The fact that I was playing the part of the Christmas star didn't bother me in the least. Everyone knew the importance of this particular star, and how it led the three wise men to Jesus.

I told everyone who was willing to listen about my "starring" role. It never occurred to me that it was Jesus who was the real star. After all, Jesus was played by a month-old baby who slept throughout the entire performance.

Not me. I stood center stage in my glittery costume and spoke my lines without missing a cue. I even remembered to project as my teacher, Mrs.

Simpson, had instructed, and to blink my eyes to give the impression of "twinkling."

It wasn't until years later that I learned that the most important things in life aren't necessarily the ones on center stage. Nor are they the ones that glitter or make the most noise.

Santa Claus commands top billing with our children, but he's not what Christmas is about. Nor is it about presents, toys or even parties. Yet you would never believe this by the elaborate commercials on TV.

In this world of bigger and better, it's difficult to keep things in perspective. The glitter of Christmas can be blinding. If the mountain of presents upstages the nativity scene, and the Church stays in the wings, how can we hope to teach our little ones the true meaning of the holiday season? If more time is spent singing "Frosty the Snowman" than "Silent Night," can we really blame our youngsters for not recognizing the real "star" of Christmas?

Lord, help us not to be dazzled by glitter or distracted by commercialism. Grant us the wisdom and strength to keep you in the spotlight, not only at Christmas, but all year 'round. Amen.

In God's Care

ANNETTE PARRISH

*The Spirit helps us in our weakness. We do
not know what we ought to pray for, but the
Spirit himself intercedes for us with groans
that words cannot express.* Romans 8:26, *NIV*

It seems I spent every summer of my 20s
in the hospital. I had several brushes with uterine
cancer, four miscarriages and three difficult pregnancies. Yet, the pregnancies were successful, and the
struggles seemed worth it. I thanked God that despite
my poor health, I'd been blessed with Anna, Aimee
and Melissa.

Now the spots on my uterus had returned and it
seemed I could no longer delay a hysterectomy.
There was some concern that I could tolerate surgery, however. I had contracted a serious lung infection called Valley Fever during my pregnancy with
Aimee. It had been complicated by pneumonia and I
had to stay in bed the last five months before her
delivery. The infection badly scarred my lungs; I lost

a third of my breathing capacity. This could complicate my ability to withstand anesthesia.

Before surgery could be attempted, I had to check into the hospital for tests. Among these was a chest x-ray.

The doctor walked into the room without looking up. Wanting to put him at ease, I began, "It's really not as bad as it looks on film. You see, I recovered from a rather nasty bout with Valley Fever and my lungs are scarred—but I feel fine!"

"You never had Valley Fever," he said. "You can get dressed now."

Stunned, I argued with him for 15 minutes. "You've mixed up my x-rays with someone else's," I protested. Although he insisted they were mine, he finally agreed to take another picture.

After half an hour, the doctor returned. He slapped the new x-ray against a lighted backdrop so I could see it, and declared, vindicated, "As I said, your chest x-ray is beautifully clear. I don't know who told you you had Valley Fever, but he or she was wrong. You never see lungs this pristine with even a mild case."

I explained that I had gone through all the blood tests and diagnostic procedures. They had all been positive. I invited him to call my regular physician.

"That won't be necessary," he said disgustedly. "I've really given this more time than I should have already. Your lungs are in excellent shape. You should be able to tolerate anesthesia well."

What's going on? I wondered. I remembered the months in bed, the fevers and coughing spells. I had been so afraid that I would lose my baby. I'd struggled and prayed for her safety.

Then it struck me. Although I had prayed for Aimee, not for myself, *someone else had.* I had been healed. There seemed to be no other explanation. I hadn't felt a warmth or tingle or any other special sensation. But there were the x-rays. My ravaged lungs were fresh and pink as a baby's.

Thank you, Lord, for giving me the Holy Spirit, who prays for me when I don't know what I should pray for or when I forget to ask for your help. Amen.

Cloud Array
MARIA METLOVA-KEARNS

I'm glad to have been alone today
And let my fancy play at will,
To watch billowing clouds in gold array
Adorn in joy the distant hill
And slowly, sweetly fade away.

Yet leave a picture that will not fade,
Unfailing peace my heart doth find,
As angel faces form clouds heaven-
made
And of His perfect love, they do
remind
We can worship God unafraid.

Flying High

BARBARA HYATT

*Look at the birds! They don't worry about what
to eat . . . for your heavenly Father feeds them.
And you are far more valuable to him than they
are.* Matthew 6:26, *TLB*

One winter I worked as secretary and
receptionist at a mortuary. I had smiled my way
through the interview and had gotten the job, but it
hadn't taken me long to realize that it was going to be
a real challenge. Not only did I have to answer the
phone calls of the bereaved in a loving yet profes-
sional manner—there was that big IBM typewriter! I
had taken the job, praying I could handle it.

My husband had just been affected by a large company layoff, so I had needed to work. One particularly
dark and dreary day I sat all by myself in the large
office of the mortuary. While I typed a letter, my
thoughts drifted to the house payment and utility
bills. I soon felt overwhelmed. Tears came as I
thought about the fact that we also needed groceries.
Furthermore, Christmas was coming.

Suddenly, my thoughts were interrupted by a noise at the window. I walked over to see what it was. Through my tears, I saw that a sparrow had flown into the window and, stunned by the blow, had fallen to the ground.

This little incident reminded me of what God has to say in His Word about the birds of the air. He's aware of and provides for all of their needs. How much more is He aware of His children in need.

I felt so encouraged as I recalled sermons on this topic. I could almost hear the gospel singer: "His Eye Is On the Sparrow." I hummed the song the rest of the day. My faith increased, as I learned to trust God for my every need.

Then one morning a friend stood at the front door. "The Lord laid it on my heart to give you this money," he said. He didn't know it, but it was our house payment. Later, several checks came in the mail from a loving friend, signed, "Love, Jesus." One week we were invited out to dinner every night. And the children ended up having a delightful Christmas.

How wonderful it is to have a heavenly Father who not only sees to the needs of the birds of the air, but to each one of His children.

Thank you, Lord, that when all else seems to fall in around me, you reach down and provide my every need. And thank you for the blessings of loving friends who show your tender loving care. Amen.

My Hiding Place

BERIT KJOS

You are my hiding place; you will protect me from trouble and surround me with songs of deliverance. Psalm 32:7, NIV

Outside my kitchen window, four children played hide-and-seek. I had to laugh at some of their funny hiding places.

Years ago, I played their game. Into my mind flashed hiding places that felt cozy enough to sleep in. Others were cramped, cold and hard. *Like some of the strange places God selects for His children,* I thought.

My hiding place in God, the place where His love guards me, may seem dismal or delightful. Pleasant or painful for the moment, it fits His plan for my protection and growth. There I am safe from stalking enemies such as fatigue, pressures, pride and cravings. He has promised to keep me safe, holy, separated unto Himself; and He does, in His chosen places.

My King may use any part of His creation to shelter me. By hiding Jonah for three days in the belly of a great fish, He provided safety from the sea, proof of His sovereignty, and transportation to Jonah's place of ministry. By hiding Israel 400 grueling years in Egypt, God unified His people and guarded them from corruption in Canaan.

I trust that He will always choose the hiding place that best prepares me for tomorrow. It may not look or feel like a hiding place in God, but when I rest in it, my King accomplishes His purpose.

"I will give you the treasures of darkness," He assures me, "riches stored in secret places, so that you may know that I am the Lord" (Isa. 45:3, *NIV*).

Each day I have a choice. I can accept God's provision, or run from Him. When I choose Him, He hides me in the secret place of His presence. What could be better?

Suddenly, the door flew open and four hungry kids burst in. "Have some cookies," I laughed, "and let me tell you what God showed me while you were playing."

Keep me hidden in you, precious Lord. Guard me from presumptuous confidence that would tempt me to leave the safety of your hiding place for me. Thank you, my King. Amen.

Time to Dry Their Tears

DAWN DULAINE

There is a time for everything, and a
season for every activity under heaven.
Ecclesiastes 3:1, *NIV*

I can hear my pillow calling me," I said, going up the last flight of stairs to my cabin. It had been a long day. I was serving as staff to 29 kids on the mercy ship *Anastasis.*

We had been traveling for four weeks, taking the gospel of Jesus, along with medical care and other relief, to Third World countries.

That night, as I opened the door to the cabin I shared with four of the kids, my mind was only on how good my bed was going to feel. But there, on the couch curled up with her pillow, sat one of the girls. Looking at my watch, I had a sinking feeling that this night was going to be longer than I had anticipated. It was already 11:30.

"I can't get to sleep," my young cabin mate sighed.

I had a decision to make. I could tell her I was too tired and would talk to her in the morning, or I could stop and really try to show her God's love and caring.

I plopped down and put my arms around her. Then the tears began to fall from her eyes. She wept as she told me the tragic news of her day. She had called home only to find that her mother was leaving her father for another man.

"What am I going to do?" she cried.

As we talked into the wee hours of the night, I sensed God's presence and His loving hand upon her.

"God, I know that Mom is confused," she prayed. "I pray against the devil's schemes. I am claiming victory over her life and I will not give her up to his evil. I love her, Jesus. Amen."

We looked at each other and hugged, then we said good night.

Lord, thanks for showing me that a little discomfort now is nothing in light of eternity. May I always be sensitive to those around me. Amen.

The Right Foundation

JESSICA C. ERRICO

*And the rain descended, and the floods came,
and the winds blew, and burst against that
house; and yet it did not fall, for it had been
founded upon the rock. Matthew 7:25, NASB*

Wait! Before you cut it down, I want to
get my camera!" I told the man from the public utility
who was readying his saw.

He shot me a quizzical look as if to say, "Lady,
who in their right mind would take a picture of a top-
pled tree?"

Returning with the camera, I examined the
uprooted young tree that threatened to damage the
utility lines in front of my home. A wind storm had
caused the sapling to lose its footing in the majestic
stump, where it had grown from a pine cone. Now it

leaned precariously against some neighboring branches at a 45-degree angle, roots exposed.

The massive stump, once a nourishing foundation for the young tree, had been decaying for some time. A large clump of it hung in the air, still grasped by the clinging roots. The strong outward appearance of the old stump was so deceiving.

For eight years, my family and I enjoyed the idyllic picture of the sapling sprouting from the dignified stump. But overnight, the scene lost its beauty and wonder, becoming a dangerous situation. The parallels to Christ's teaching were obvious.

I remembered Jesus teaching the multitudes about the kind of foundation they should build their lives on. He used the parable of a man building his house on a rock, a solid foundation.

Jesus said that when we hear His words and put them into practice we will be strongly supported and survive the storms that threaten. However, a life not built on God's truth, like the house of a foolish man built on sand, will crash in the face of trials and adversities.

The predicament in my front yard illustrated the consequences of choosing the wrong foundation. Worldly values based on educational honors, job promotions, designer clothes and expensive homes appear attractive on the outside. Yet they are as sand to the life that is not built on Jesus and His words.

By the time I adjusted the light meter and focused the lens, my neighbors had gathered, waiting to see the tree come down. With a "click" I captured the living parable. Everyone hesitated a moment, and I knew I should share my faith. Boldly, I explained, "This uprooted tree reminds me that I need Jesus to be my foundation. Nothing else can support me forever!"

Please, Lord, be my foundation. Though the things of this world try to distract me, keep me rooted in your words. Thank you, Jesus! Amen.

A Fresh New Day
SHIRLEY MITCHELL

The early morning sunlight
Spreads its rays across the sky.
Like great golden fingers,
Making my spirits fly so high!

The brightness of God's sunlight
Cheers my soul and warms my
bones.
What a magnificent creation
God's great beauty to behold!

God says to me in the stillness,
"Feed my lambs with great delight.
In a world that's filled with
darkness,
I want you to be my sunlight!"

Love that Won't Let Go

DARLENE SYBERT ANDREE

For I am convinced that neither death, nor life, nor angels, nor principalities, nor things present, nor things to come, . . . nor any other created thing, shall be able to separate us from the love of God. Romans 8:38,39, *NASB*

For two weeks, the four of us had shared the warm sunshine of August in western Washington and the fun of being together: my two grown sons, my sister and I. It was our first such experience in many years, since my older son has been with the Army in Texas and my other son has been attending college. In addition, my sister lives 1,200 miles away.

But, by God's grace, schedules and finances had meshed so that we could have this special time to get reacquainted. We played Trivial Pursuit and Pictionary late into the night. We hiked on Mount Rainier and wandered through Seattle's Pick Place Market and Pioneer Square. We shared ideas about

145

God, science, politics and relationships. We discussed books we've read and books we want to read.

All too quickly the time was gone and we had to separate. It was painful to part, knowing it would be months, maybe years, before we might all be together again.

That experience made the words of God's love in Romans 8:38,39 even more precious. How reassuring it is to know that nothing can ever separate us from His love. He has given His Son to redeem us, His Spirit to comfort and guide us, and He has promised to be with us always.

Because He has given so freely and completely, I know that He is willing and able to keep me in His love forever. I can accept the circumstances of my life, even the partings from my human family and friends, because I know there will be no separation from Him and His love.

Father, teach me to be joyful and full of thanks in all circumstances, knowing that because Christ lives in me and I in Him, I will never be separated from your love. Amen.

Labor Till the Harvest

DEBBIE KALMBACH

*Let us not become weary in doing good, for at
the proper time we will reap a harvest if we do
not give up.* Galatians 6:9, NIV

"I quit!" Tears streamed uncontrollably
down my face. My husband cradled my heaving
shoulders and allowed the torrent of emotion to flow.

It had been two months since the knee surgery,
and now it was time for the painful task of rehabilita-
tion. But my knee refused to bend. Day after day the
therapists stretched and tugged on my leg without
progress. It was agony.

"I can't go back," I sobbed. "It hurts too much."
Just thinking about the next session made my stom-
ach churn.

Even as I protested, I knew I had choices. I could
give up, refusing to endure any more pain. Then my

147

knee would never improve. I'd be crippled. I needed to muster enough courage to keep going, though it was extremely difficult.

Finally, after many weeks of therapy, the stiffness eased and my knee was bending.

How often I encounter other circumstances in life when I want to give up. I grow weary of praying for seemingly impossible situations and, when prayers go unanswered, I become discouraged. It hurts too much to continue loving, to keep on doing good when results can't be clearly seen. Many times I've cried out, "I quit! I can't handle any more."

Then I'm reminded of my choices. I can give up, refusing to endure the pain of adversity. Or I can keep going, by faith, believing that any effort that is God-honoring is never in vain. Like my knee, when I choose to persevere, at the proper time a harvest is reaped.

Dear Lord, thank you for your faithfulness, for never giving up on me. Help me to keep going when I'd rather quit. Amen.

Safe in the Savior's Hand

ANNA HAYFORD

Even there Thy hand will lead me,
and Thy right hand will lay hold of me.
Psalm 139:10, *NASB*

It was her first day of school, our little surprise bundle of joy, and, as was my custom with all of our children, I walked with her. She was seven years behind our older children; a lot had changed in the schools. Besides, we had moved and were in a new school district.

Of course, we had prayed together before we left the house. Daddy said his special prayer for the first day of school. But still I felt uneasy.

As we entered her classroom, my unrest became reality as I noted her teacher's jewelry. It was a large

149

amulet on a silver chain and I didn't like the looks of the figure on it.

Walking home alone, I again asked the Lord to watch over her. I felt as though I was throwing my little child to the wolves.

The next day I again walked my daughter to school. I was surprised to hear music filling the room as we entered. My heart soared when I heard the words to "He's Got the Whole World in His Hands."

This time, as I walked home, I thanked the Lord for His care of Christa. He whispered in my ear, "I did that just for you. Don't you know that since you dedicated her to me when she was a baby, I would continually hold her in my hand? You cannot be with her every moment; *but I can, and I will.*"

From that day on, I rested in the Lord concerning my daughter, knowing she was being taken care of in a way only our loving heavenly Father could.

Dear Lord Jesus, I am so thankful that I can trust my children into your care. Bless each one daily, helping them to trust you, too. And may your name always be glorified through them. Amen.

In His Time

LINDA MONTOYA

*Now glory be to God who by his mighty power
at work within us is able to do far more than
we would ever dare to ask or even dream of—
infinitely beyond our highest prayers, desires,
thoughts, or hopes.* Ephesians 3:20, *TLB*

The old piece of paper lying in the street
caught my eye. I picked it up and read Ephesians
3:20. Over and over I read the words. Soon, hope
began to replace the discouragement I had been feeling because we had not been able to buy a house.

Prices in Southern California were escalating so
fast, it seemed there was no way to catch up. Now
this verse gave me tremendous encouragement that
the Lord, indeed, had a home for us.

I began praising Him for the house He would provide. I praised Him for the yard that would be big
enough for a swing set and a doll house, and for the
family room that would be large enough for a pool
table. Day after day, I visualized myself walking
through my house. As I did, I talked with the Lord,

praising and thanking Him for all that He was preparing for us.

A whole year had gone by when my friend Ann called. Her sister-in-law had a house for sale, and Ann thought it would be perfect for us. Even though the price was way out of reach, my husband, Frank, said, "Let's go look at it!"

Approaching the house, we were impressed by the yard. Then we noticed the pool table through the window of the family room. Even before entering, Frank said, "We'll take it!"

The owner came down on the price and provided secondary financing. Within hours we had signed the contract.

Exciting details then began to unfold. The owners decided to leave the doll house and swing set. The carpet matched our furniture. Many more of the very things I had praised God for over a year ago were coming to pass. And day after day we saw how God had truly given us this home.

Almighty God and Father, thank you for your provisions. Help me to see by the power of your Holy Word how I can reach the altitudes you have designed for me. Amen.

He Keeps His Promises!

ZOE B. METZGER

I will send down the showers in their season;
they shall be showers of blessing.
Ezekiel 34:26, *RSV*

My first grandchild. A little girl. How thrilled I was! How perfect she seemed. I was on cloud nine, anticipating her first smile, her first steps, her first words. We'd pick flowers together and catch colors from rainbows. I'd show her all God's wonders and teach her to sing about them.

Then came the heartaches. She was blind and deaf, the tragic consequence of German measles suffered by her mother, early in pregnancy. Despair engulfed me. "Father, in heaven, why? Why?" But God didn't seem to answer me. No visions appeared, no still small voice could be heard. I had but His Word and His promise from Romans 8:28 that all that happens to us is for our good, if we love Him.

That was 18 years ago. That baby girl is now a lovely young woman and there is nothing tragic about her. Surgery has given her limited sight. She knows my face, and her artistic hands draw sweet likenesses of flowers and rainbows. With fluent sign language, she shares with me her hopes and dreams. We laugh and joke, we sing and pray. She is a blessing!

Our gracious Father has taken care of her very well. I should have known He would. After all, He promised!

Lord, thank you for the heartaches you send us. Help us to leave them in your loving care. Amen.

Child of the King

RHONDA McGARRAH

*For you have not received a spirit of slavery
leading to fear again, but you have received a
spirit of adoption as sons by which we cry out,
"Abba, Father!"* Romans 8:15, *NASB*

s I knelt down on my knees to pray, my
heartfelt request was, "Show me your love, God, your
unconditional love. I want to know you as my Abba,
Father, my daddy."

Many hard and painful circumstances had
brought me to this point. Some emotional healing
had been taking place in my life over the last few
months, but I really wanted to understand God's
love. I wanted to be free of feeling like I always had to
be good enough to earn it.

I knew that God's love was available; I'd studied
His Word for years. I knew godly Christian women
who understood the love of God; they seemed to be at

such peace with Him. I could even teach others about it, and I believed it. But I couldn't feel it. The feeling of total acceptance by the one who loves you, no matter what you do, eluded me. I needed to get the head knowledge of God's truths down into my heart.

That day, my prayer brought a precious moment into my life, one I'll never forget. My loving, heavenly Father brought to mind a picture of Himself on the throne with all the kings of the nations standing before Him, busily bringing up the problems of the world. I came running through the crowd, calling, "Daddy, Daddy!" He put His hands out as if to quiet the others, then held His arms open wide to me. I jumped right up onto His lap, and He wrapped His protective arms around me and held me close.

I was His biggest priority, and He had time for me. I was—and still am—His beloved child.

Oh, Lord, thank you that you love me unconditionally. I will love you with all my heart, too. I am so grateful that even when I am unfaithful or unlovable, you remain faithful and loving. Amen.

I'm Parched, Lord

GAY LEWIS

Come, all you who are thirsty, come to the waters. Isaiah 55:1, *NIV*

I was upset. We'd had yet another late night, and now my husband had just rushed off for five days out of town. It was 5:30 A.M. The week ahead loomed heavy with responsibility, and I had an awful headache.

I began prowling tiredly around the house, making it mine again after several days away. I watered plants, picked off dead leaves and doctored some poor, wilted plants that a sick friend had sent home with us the day before.

One large vine was pitiful. Its leaves were still a dull green, but limp and curled.

157

"I look like that, too, don't I, Lord?" I asked wearily. "At least that's how I feel inside."

I had drenched the vine the night before, but the water had run right through the dry soil. As I stood staring at it, wondering how on earth I would ever get enough water into it, the words came into my mind. *Immerse it.* Setting the pot down into a large bowl, I poured water on the plant until the bowl and the pot were both full. In half an hour I could see the difference, and by evening almost all the leaves had uncurled and plumped up. What a miracle!

How could I possibly miss the obvious lesson? If my parched soul looked like that plant had, then the remedy must be the same: *Immerse it.*

With tears I acknowledged my failure to be still long enough to receive the living water my Lord continually offers me.

Lord, remind me to constantly immerse myself in you, and to soak up the love you pour on me. Amen.

He Never Sleeps

ALICE C. PETER

*In fact, no one can enter a strong man's house
and carry off his possessions unless he first
ties up the strong man. Then he can rob his
house.* Mark 3:27, NIV

My computer drones most of the day
and my busy life bubbles with fresh escapades as long
as there is daylight. But night comes swiftly in Seattle
and I feel a little shiver as I check my apartment door
latch, then run my finger along the metal frame to
make sure each window is locked.

I love living in downtown Seattle, where lectures
at the main library, the symphony, the ballet and art
museums are all within walking distance. But I
spend countless hours shaking under the covers at
night, wondering what I can do to keep myself safe.

The evening news carries so many stories about
robberies, stabbings and the like that I panic when a

strange noise shatters the darkness or an unfamiliar shadow presses against the wall. I am often anxious, allowing myself to climb into bed with fear and dread as my companions.

Evil lurks all around me. And I allow Satan to break down my defenses until I'm left with dread. My "house"—me, myself—is divided, bombarded with nightly bouts of negativism.

I wonder, *Are my nightly fears symptoms of a too-busy life? Am I going about my nightly ritual all wrong?*

I can check to make sure that I do not overlook the proper precautions out of carelessness. But I must not forget the one thing that casts fear from my mind—God's promise to me in Mark 3:27: "No one can enter a strong man's house and carry off his possessions unless he first ties up the strong man."

Instead of wasting time wondering what I can do to keep myself safe, I want to crawl into bed praising the Lord for His Word. If my "house" is placed into the loving arms of Jesus, I can rest in Him and sleep without fear.

Lord, Father, thank you that I can lay me down to rest knowing you never sleep, but are watching over me and keeping me from all harm. Amen.

God, Where Are You!

ANNA HAYFORD

And my God will meet all your needs according to his glorious riches in Christ Jesus.
Philippians 4:19, *NIV*

In our early years of ministry, our salary was just not stretching far enough to feed and clothe three small children. We had prayed and Jack had taken every extra speaking engagement he could; but still we were struggling with finances.

I became unhappy with God. I was happy in the ministry, but there were some things I just couldn't understand. One day I complained to Him about our life and our finances.

As I knelt I began taking issue with God. "Lord, you know we tithe, and we give offerings. We try to be careful with our money; we're good stewards of it. We have even given you our lives and serve you faithfully.

"Lord, why are there people everywhere who don't love you, who don't serve you, who don't tithe, yet they seem to have all the money they need or want, while we have to watch every penny?"

With the tenderness only a loving Father can give, He impressed me with this thought: *They don't get to trust me, either.*

Those were the only words He spoke to me, but suddenly I realized how very privileged I was. *I got to trust the Lord!*

If those others, who seem to have everything, were in my shoes, where would they turn? In whom could they trust?

Oh, Lord, I am so blessed to be able to trust you. Thank you for pointing out my place of enthronement by your side. I know that you will never leave me nor forsake me, that every provision I need will be mine. Thank you, too, for being so tender with your correction. Make me an obedient and uncomplaining child. Amen.

A Choir Robe and a Gag?

MARTHA BOLTON

His lord said unto him, Well done, thou good
and faithful servant: thou hast been faithful
over a few things, I will make thee ruler over
many things: enter thou into the joy of thy
lord. Matthew 25:21, *KJV*

I'm not what you'd call a singer. In fact, I'm not what anyone would call a singer. Oh, they've let me join the choir at church, but I have to face the opposite direction. Our conductor did give me a solo once, but unfortunately it came at the exact moment the entire congregation got up to get a drink of water.

I've always loved the story of the talents in Matthew 25. Whether the workers got five talents, two or one, the owner's point was to put them to use. The first time I heard the story, it made a great impact, and I determined that whatever talents I'd been given would be used for the Lord.

If they asked me to play the piano, I was going to

163

do it. If they asked me to lead a children's choir, I'd say, "When do I start?" If they asked me to sing at our annual church camp, I'd be up at the microphone in a second. Above all else, I wanted to be willing.

But they didn't ask me to do any of those things. What they did ask me to do was direct the Christmas play.

"The what?"

"The Christmas play," my pastor explained. "In fact, why don't you write one for us?"

So for once I didn't even think about all the musical talents I had to offer the Lord. I merely did what my pastor asked: I wrote a Christmas play. And I loved it! Better yet, the audience loved it. They laughed. They cried.

Now there was no stopping me. I volunteered to write everything from the church newsletter to Mother's and Father's Day programs to letters to our missionaries. Whatever department needed words, I'd provide them. I'd take telephone messages for our pastor and deliver them in essay form. Simple attendance records turned into individual theses on church growth. And we had the first visitor's cards that ever came out in hardback.

Had I, at last, found something I could do? Had the Lord finally given me a talent? No, it was always there. I was just so busy comparing myself to five- and two-talent people I didn't think He could do anything with my one.

But I was wrong. The beautiful thing about God's family is that we're all needed—some to sing, some to play the piano, some to teach and some to write.

Oh, but don't get me wrong. I haven't given up on my singing. In fact, choir practice is Thursday night and I plan to go. Now if I could just get someone to tell me where they're meeting.

Dear Lord, let me always be willing to serve you with whatever talents you've given me. Amen.

First published in *Christian Herald,* December, 1987.

This Day
GLORIA GAITHER

There is beauty in the morning
   With the sun tip-toeing in,
When the day's a brand new conscience
   And the world's a chance to win.

There is muscle in the noontime
   When the sun is plowing through
Hot and bright and clear and brawny,
   Nature's time to go and do.

There's a charm about the evening—
   Gentle, loving like a friend,
Smiling o'er the west horizon,
   Tying up the day's loose ends.

Lovely, complicated wrappings
   Sheath the gift of one-day-more;
Breathless, I untie the package—
   Never lived *this* day before!

From *Let's Make a Memory,* by Gloria Gaither and Shirley Dobson, copyright 1983. Published by Word Books. Used by permission.

Seeing Jesus

BERIT KJOS

Be still, and know that I am God.
Psalm 46:10, *KJV*

T ake off your shoes, for this is holy ground."

As quietly as she spoke, Kay knelt on the rug by the coffee table and slipped off her sandals. Quickly, I followed her example.

Then, the little white-haired disciple began to talk with her best Friend. Her words brought indelible images of my King. I saw my Father holding me in His gentle embrace, my Shepherd waiting for me to come near and follow, my Warrior fighting my every battle. To this conquering King, Kay carried all the concerns we had shared. I felt I had entered into another dimension of life—indeed, I had! And I didn't want to leave.

An hour earlier, I had rung the bell and waited by

Kay's front door, hope and fear mingling in my mind. *If God would only let me be her friend. But how could someone so special want to spend time with me?* Silently I had sung a prayer to my King: *Make me a blessing.* I knew *I* would be blessed. Kay had invited me for lunch, but I hungered to know how to grow, meditate, become like Jesus, rest in His will. Many gave answers, but Kay lived them.

I had come as a new Christian, with a multitude of questions. With quiet sensitivity, Kay answered each one, always pointing me to Jesus and His Word. Full of wonder, I listened, so aware of God's holiness and wisdom in Kay. Unhurried, we read and prayed His Word; every verse came straight from His heart to our. Then we gave it back. Finally, we knelt together—without shoes.

Kay's friendship through the years continues to remind me to slow down, to talk, walk and work with the quiet dignity befitting a bride of the King. She reminds me to rest in my Shepherd's pastures and meditate on His Word, giving it time to root and grow in my heart. Through her I hear the gentle voice of my King whispering, "Be still, and know that I am God."

Precious Jesus, continue to touch me with your stillness whenever daily demands dim my vision. Keep me so close to you that my life will remind others to be quiet enough to see, hear, love and follow you. Thank you, my beloved King. Amen.

The Maternity Dress

DARLENE HOFFA

Forget the former things; do not dwell on the past. Isaiah 43:18, *NIV*

How beautiful!" my sister said, as she pulled back the tissue surrounding the red and white gingham maternity dress I had bought for her. Expecting her third child, she was delighted with something new to wear. She wore it as often as she could keep it washed and ironed.

"*You* borrow it!" my sister teased. "I'm finished with maternity dresses." As I carried our first child, I enjoyed wearing the dress my sister had appreciated so much. I wore it as often as I could keep it washed and ironed.

"You're not going to wear that thing again with this baby!" my husband joked. Now that I was expecting my second child, I saw the dress as part of our family tradition. It didn't need to be ironed after washing; the dress was too tired to hold a wrinkle.

Weeks later, my husband came home from work to find the maternity dress lying on the bed. "You don't need to wear that red and white disaster one more time!" he laughed. "Let's get you some new clothes tomorrow. I'll go with you." He marched to the trash barrel and tore the dress into tiny little strips. He knew this dress was too revered to ever become a dust cloth.

I could never have parted with that maternity dress if he hadn't taken drastic action. Part of me loves to hang on to the familiar. Without my husband's help, I clutch people, places and routines to me, long after a change would be far better.

Giving up that worn out dress reminds me how many times since then that God has said, "You don't need that any more. Let's get you some new adventures tomorrow. I'll go with you."

And He always does.

Dear Lord, while I treasure my past, I want to move forward into the future. Teach me to view each day as a surprise gift, about to be opened with your help. Amen.

Going the Distance

MARLA HILL

*Do you not know that in a race all the runners
compete, but only one receives the prize?
So run that you may obtain it.*
1 Corinthians 9:24, RSV

Our daughter had decided to quit the cross-country team. The glory she had imagined turned out to be mostly hard work and very little glory.

My husband and I decided we would be poor parents to let her quit before giving it a good try. We saw in the "long run," the goal of sticking with something until the end, and then the beauty in achieving that goal. It didn't matter if she became the best on the team.

We loved her too much to want her to learn to give up, and lovingly gave her our decision. She was furious with us, and sure that we couldn't possibly understand. She stomped away with, "I hate you!" Her words stung. My heart was breaking. But I knew what she was really saying was, "I hate what you're making me go through; I hate that I can't have my way in this matter!"

How often do I say the same thing to the Lord, only in different words? "Why must I endure this pain, Lord? You can't possibly understand. Just let me quit this time, Lord."

My words hurt Him. They break His heart. But my heavenly Father loves me too much to let me quit. He knows that in the long run I will be stronger in my faith, and in my walk and relationship with Him.

It wasn't long before our daughter nestled herself into our laps to ask forgiveness. And so it is with us. When we argue with God and want to quit before we reach our desired goal, we can nestle in His loving arms and ask forgiveness, and for strength to go the distance.

Lord, forgive me when I disagree with your plan for my life. Help me to run the good race, as I watch the plan you have for me unfold. Amen.

Blossoms in His Eyes

EILEEN HEGEL

For we are unto God a sweet savour of Christ,
in them that are saved, and in them that
perish. 2 Corinthians 2:15, *KJV*

A girlfriend of mine views women as flowers that show forth the beauty of the Lord. Roses, carnations, lilies, sunflowers, daffodils—all are fragrances in God's garden of delight. I've always liked this analogy, because I love fresh flowers; they add vitality to life, brighten up my day, make me smile.

I remember asking a man I was going out with, "If you could see me as a flower, what would I be?" You can imagine his response—no comment, just a rather strange look.

The next day my girlfriend phoned. I wanted so much to ask her what kind of flower she thought I was. I didn't dare. But moments later she said, "By the way, I want to tell you what kind of flower you are."

"You do?" I replied.

"Yes," she said. "I think you're a carnation."

"Why a carnation?" I asked, disappointed. I wanted to be an elegant, fragrant rose.

"Because carnations are sweet and strong!" she answered.

I hung up the phone feeling like I had just been pruned. "Hey, God," I shouted. "I can't even think of one carnation that smells that great!"

A few weeks later someone gave me a bouquet of carnations. "Not funny, God," I said. Then, as I drove home, I grew to like my carnations. They were quite lovely. And I noticed they even smelled a little spicy. And then I heard Him say, "That's because you're beginning to like yourself."

"You're right, God," I whispered, "Spicy. Yeah, that's me. I like adding a little zest to life."

I'm so glad I've allowed God to open up the petals of my heart. He cares for me and wants to replace hurt, anger, bitterness and resentment with His love and sweet aroma. He cares for me.

What kind of flower are you? He sees each one of us as His most precious blossoms, you know!

Father, thank you for seeing me as a beautiful flower in your garden of delight. May I reach out to others with the sweet fragrance of your son Jesus Christ. Amen.

You're a What?

SHERYL HAYSTEAD

See how great a love the Father has bestowed upon us, that we should be called children of God. 1 John 3:1, *NASB*

Recently I read an article entitled "You Know You're a Mother When. . . . " It listed 17 ways to prove one's motherhood—ways like knowing all the words to "The Itsy-Bitsy Spider," having a bathtub filled with little yellow duckies and other assorted bath toys, finding yourself using an old cloth diaper as a dust rag.

What would the list be like if the title was "You Know You're a *Christian* When . . . "? My list has changed several times over the years. As a child I might have said, "When you go to Sunday School every week," or "When you pray before every meal." In my teen years my responses would have dealt

174

more with a vague acknowledgment of belief in God. Efforts to evangelize the world (or at least my college campus) was the mark of a Christian in my college years.

Today, knowing I'm a Christian still has to do with fellowship at my church, prayer on a regular basis, belief in God and sharing my faith. But no longer is it enough to say I know I'm a Christian because I attend church every Sunday or pray at mealtimes.

Perhaps, just as a woman knows she's a mother because of that special bond between her and a certain child, the key to knowing I'm a Christian is in that unique bond between myself and my Savior.

Routine times of learning and worship with a believing community have become experiences of faith and renewal. Daily, the God in whom I once expressed vague belief reveals more of the riches of His character. And in the challenge to share the good news of Christ with others in my neighborhood, I find the fruit of that early desire to evangelize.

My house—not to mention my car, my yard and my schedule—show plenty of evidence that I'm a mother. I'm looking each day, however, for that special one-of-a-kind evidence that shows I'm part of God's family.

I'm grateful, Father, that I belong to you. Help me as I daily seek to strengthen the bond between us. Amen.

Treasured Memories

SHIRLEY DOBSON

"Mary treasured up all these things and pondered them in her heart." Luke 2:19, *NIV*

On Christmas Eve each year, we enjoy a dinner of Chinese food. (Don't ask me how that tradition started, or more important, why?) Afterwards, grandparents, aunts, uncles and cousins join us around the fireplace, and my husband, Jim, reads from the Bible. After discussing the passage, we do something very meaningful.

The lights are lowered and I give each family member a votive candle. I explain as we take our turn igniting our candle that the light represents Jesus who was born into a dark world to give us eternal life. As each person lights his candle, he shares one blessing he is especially thankful for during the past year, and something he or she is asking God to do in his life the following year—perhaps a spiritual goal for the coming year. We then blow out our candles

176

and Jim closes in prayer. The children then get to select and open one gift from under the tree.

Those happy days of Christmas come and go so quickly that we have sought a way to hold on to the pleasure a while longer. Therefore, we have developed a custom of saving our Christmas cards from friends and loved ones far and wide. After New Year's Day, I put them on a tray near the dinner table. Every night we select four cards, one for each family member, and we read them and the enclosed letters. We then pray for those families around our table. This tradition may take months to complete, depending on the number of cards we receive. With the busy days of Christmas behind us, we can better enjoy the beauty of the cards, and absorb the meaningful verses and personal notes.

The Christmas traditions we have developed through the years are not unique to the Dobson household. Perhaps yours are similar in many respects. But they are extremely meaningful to each member of our family. These activities serve to emphasize the two vitally important themes that embody the Christmas spirit: celebration of Jesus' birth and life, and celebration of love for one another and for the entire human family.

Heavenly Father, how we treasure the memory of your Son's birth so many years ago. Thank you for ways to pass these memories on to our children and to keep the birth of Jesus and His life alive in our hearts today! Amen.

Adapted from *Let's Make a Memory* by Shirley Dobson and Gloria Gaither, copyright 1983. Published by Word Books. Used by permission.

Love, God

MARGARET BROWNLEY

Yet hear the word of the Lord.
Jeremiah 9:20, *KJV*

The bouquet arrived early one gloomy morning in September—a dozen red roses nestled in a cloud of baby's breath. It wasn't my birthday, nor any other occasion I could think of. What would warrant such a gift?

Reaching for the tiny envelope on the plastic holder, I quickly pulled out the card.

Two words greeted my startled eyes. Thinking I was mistaken, I blinked and stared again at the big, bold handwriting. The card read, *Love, God.*

My Christian upbringing had instilled in me a firm belief in God's love, but I never expected Him to send me a personal reminder. Especially now.

Recently, I had felt distant from God. Financial, health and family concerns had taken their toll. I felt drained and exhausted. It was as if I were trying to hold back an avalanche.

Love, God.

It was amazing what power those two little words had. But who could have sent the roses? And why?

As I questioned family and friends, one by one, they all denied sending the roses and seemed as curious as I. Who was the secret donor?

Love, God.

The roses seemed to fill the house; their delicate fragrance followed me from room to room. It suddenly occurred to me as I rifled through the bills, which had arrived that day in the mail, that I had been so busy trying to stay afloat I hadn't stopped to "smell the flowers." I had focused so much attention on the things we'd lost that I had forgotten how many wonderful blessings were still ours.

Love, God.

I suddenly found myself humming for the first time in months. My burdens were as great as ever, but they felt lighter. The roses reminded me that I didn't have to carry the load alone.

It was months later before my younger son, Darin, admitted to sending the roses. I hadn't recognized his handwriting because of an arm injury that forced him to write with his left hand.

"But why did you sign the card, *Love, God*?" I asked.

Darin had always been the skeptical one—the one whose spiritual doubts had given me the most distress.

"I don't know, Mom. I knew you were going through tough times. Somehow the words just flowed from my pen." He grinned sheepishly. "I guess God saw fit to work through me."

New wisdom and understanding appeared on my son's face. Suddenly I realized it had been no coincidence that he'd been chosen as messenger; through those roses, God had spoken to us both.

Dear God, I know you speak to your children in many ways. Help me to keep the airwaves between us free of worldly static so that I may remain "tuned in" to your voice. Amen.

Lovest Thou Me?
GERALDINE NICHOLAS

"Lovest thou me?" I heard Him say
As I started another busy day.
"Of course I love You, Lord," I replied.
But a strange uneasiness rose inside.

At mid-day I heard His voice so near,
"Do you love Me?" He whispered so I could hear,
"Why, Lord, You know I love You," I said,
"The lambs," He asked, "have they been fed?"

At evening He came to me once more
And asked the questions just as before.
I assured Him my love was deep and pure
And I'd care for the lambs tomorrow for sure.

I really thought what I'd said was true.
To say I love you is easy to do.
But the hours had quickly swept away
And the lambs were not fed that live-long day.

God's Plans—
Our Possibilities

DEBBIE KALMBACH

"For I know the plans I have for you," declares the Lord, "plans to prosper you and not to harm you, plans to give you hope and a future." Jeremiah 29:11, NIV

Slides flashed onto the makeshift wall screen at a recent family gathering. Our son's first catch held high from the fishing pole, his six-year-old face beaming with pride. A courageous leap from the diving board into Daddy's outstretched arms. Two little boys splashing in a mud puddle, eyes bright with mischief, broad grins. What a mess! I smiled, remembering the exasperation I felt as a young mom. Scrubbing those mud-covered toddlers wasn't high on my list of priorities that summer day.

"Mom, I can't believe you let us get that dirty," one of my teens chuckled.

I laughed, but found myself blinking back tears.

Where had the years gone? Pictures hold moments in time, reminding me of days when I thought caring for small children was a forever task. There would always be diapers to change, noses to wipe, "Owies" to kiss and make better, I had thought.

The years have brought changes in my role as mother. Tiny hands no longer clutch mine as I walk through the grocery store or cross a busy street. I've even been replaced as "taxi driver" by my oldest son. I have to let go—watch the boys grow to be men. It's a joy, but scary, too.

What will it be like when I walk past his room and there's no one sitting on the floor playing the guitar or listening to music through his headphones? How will I feel when there isn't anyone to tuck in at bedtime?

"Lord," I've cried, "I've been a mother as far back as I can remember. What's next? Who am I? What plans do you have for my life? School? Career?" Sometimes I feel overwhelmed.

It's comforting to reflect on how much God cares for me. He is ever-faithful, unchanging, steadfast. He's always provided the way and this transition is no different. Being a mom doesn't end at our children's high school graduation. It just takes on a new dimension.

Dear Lord, I'm thankful for the blessings of being a mother. I pray for the courage to trust you for guidance and direction. You have the perfect plan for my life. Amen.

Homework

MARILOU FLINKMAN

*Verily I say unto you, Inasmuch as ye
have done it unto one of the least of these
my brethren, ye have done it unto me.*
Matthew 25:40, *KJV*

Homework is different from housework. Keeping a house clean, meals cooked and
clothes washed is housework. Homework involves
these things, too, but only after the important work of
life is done.

Today I planned to scrub the kitchen floor. As I
got the bucket out of the cupboard, the phone rang.
Helen's husband had been out of work for over a
month and she sounded sad and scared.

I walked around the bucket and took the roast for
tonight's supper out of the refrigerator. *We'll have hot
dogs,* I thought, wrapping the meat in aluminum foil
before delivering it to Helen's house. As long as I was
out, I might as well drop off some magazines for
Grandma Rogers in the nursing home. She told me

Rose Brandon had the flu, so I stopped by the drug store to buy a get well card.

I fell over the bucket when I got home. I picked it up as Sarah burst in the back door. "Oh, Mom, it's just awful!"

A glass of milk and a few cookies later, Sarah decided her life wouldn't end if Joan had a skirt identical to hers.

I looked at the dirty floor, quietly put the bucket in the cupboard and took a package of hot dogs out of the refrigerator.

Once again, the housework had been left undone. But what makes a house a home is the caring, not the cleaning.

When I get to heaven, I expect to find those mansions a mess. Then I'll know the angels were so busy ministering to sick souls, they didn't have time to dust under the bed.

Dear Lord, keep me ever mindful of the needs of others. Amen.

His Heart of Love

LUCILLE MOSES

When my spirit was overwhelmed within me,
Thou didst know my path. Psalm 142:3, *NASB*

Wavelets lapped lazily around my toes as I gingerly stepped along the rock strewn shore of the Sea of Galilee. Dawn was the best part of each day for me. I arose early and walked along the shore where Jesus had walked, delighting in a sense of His presence.

The trip to Israel had been wonderful, but this morning I felt oddly despondent and tears came easily. Loneliness surrounded me. Did my presence matter to anyone lately?

I walked on slowly along the shore, pausing occasionally to gaze across the lake. Then, glancing down, I saw something that made me stop—and gasp.

A white rock was perched on top of other multi-

185

colored rocks as if waiting for me to claim it. I picked it up. The velvet-soft stone lay in the palm of my hand.

I could only wonder at the original shape of this piece of granite. But the form of a heart now nestled in my hand. A heart-shaped rock!

How many years had the stone lain in the waters of Galilee, gently caressed by the waves to its present form? Why hadn't someone else claimed this prize? But the rock wasn't for them to claim, was it? God had meant it just for me!

I looked upward. "Father, thank you. How like you this is. How many years, or even centuries, have you allowed this stone to be formed into a heart? And this very morning when I desperately needed assurance of your love, you tenderly placed it in my path."

I held the rock for several moments, tracing its rounded shape with my fingers, marveling at His love.

Soon I turned back, eager to join my travelling companions. A new, exciting day beckoned to me, and I was ready for whatever it brought.

Confidence swelled within me that I, too, was held in a hand, a hand of love.

Father, help me to recognize those events in my life that you have planned to answer my needs and make me aware of your love. Amen.

My Special
Little Closet

ANNE ORTLUND

*But thou, when thou prayest, enter into thy
closet, and when thou hast shut thy door, pray
to thy Father which is in secret; and thy Father
which seeth in secret shall reward thee openly.*
Matthew 6:6, *KJV*

Everybody knows of stories about some-
one who says, "If I have a normal day, I can get by
with one hour of planning and quiet with God. But if I
have a busy day, I need at least two or more."

I have to get away from the house for these quiet
times. Of course for years I couldn't, when the children were little. But I could have, sooner than I
thought of it. As soon as Buddy was in kindergarten,
I could have slipped away from the house.

In the house I see too much to do! Don't you? I'm
having a great time in the book of Jeremiah and suddenly I think, "Did I take the synthetics out of the
dryer?" Or the phone rings. Or somebody's at the
door.

When Nels is breakfasted and put off to school, then I go to a quiet corner of a restaurant where I know no one, and there I have breakfast, plan, read and pray (I write out my prayers).

Or in pretty weather I just park the car somewhere where I'm anonymous, and sit in the car.

Or I go to a secluded couch in the nook of a hotel.

For everyone, God will give a spot. But if you're stuck at home for now, vow not to answer the phone or the doorbell. Turn your chair to the corner of the room if you must. Shut out the world! Jesus called it entering into your closet. For you, that may be the bathroom.

The quality of your life will be determined by the amount of time you spend alone with God in reading, praying and planning.

Thank you, Lord, for my own little closet where I can be alone with you. Help me to set aside time everyday to bring my thoughts and prayers to you. Amen.

Adapted from *Disciplines of the Beautiful Woman,* by Anne Ortlund, copyright 1977, 1984; used by permission of Word Books, publisher.

Soup till Jesus Comes

MARGE REARICK

*Consider the ravens: They do not sow or reap,
they have no storeroom or barn; yet God feeds
them. And how much more valuable you are
than birds! Luke 12:24, NIV*

I feel the Lord would have me get off welfare," Janey said. Stunned, the rest of us turned and
stared at her.

"Me, too," blurted Susan. Becky shyly agreed.
Finally, feeling the pressure to conform, I said, "I feel
it's time to give it up, too!"

It was 1970. We were all brand new Christians,
living together in a Christian home. We had all known
each other long before we met Christ; we had lived
through the hippy scene and partied with the
"Angels." We even worked the strip together.

Someone suggested we call our pastor, just to

make sure. Poor old Pastor Rick. He hardly knew what to do with us all—a bunch of single moms, former prostitutes and drug addicts. He simply said, "Do whatever the Lord would have you do."

Next, we called Miss Jones, our case worker. She was a kindly old woman who pitied us all. But she never made us feel guilty. And she had an honest concern for our kids.

We baked our best cookies, brewed our best coffee and had Miss Jones over, so we could tell her the good news—that Jesus was going to take care of us and that we didn't need help anymore.

Suspicious, she listened to our story. Then she smiled and said, "Now you girls have to think of the children, too. After all, how will they eat?"

In perfect harmony we chimed in, "The Lord will provide."

Back and forth this exchange went, but we always countered with, "The Lord will provide."

Finally, Miss Jones gave up. She just looked at us with pity in her eyes. We all sat there in silence.

Just then, there was a knock at the door. Standing on the porch was a guy in overalls. As I opened the door, he said, "Well, where do you want it all?"

"All what?" I asked.

"Well, I've got a thousand cans of soup to deliver every three weeks, until Jesus comes. That's the message I got. I'm not supposed to tell you who it's from. I'm not even supposed to tell you why. I'm just supposed to bring them here every three weeks. Where do you want me to put them?"

Whenever I fear how God is going to take us through a new decision, ministry opportunity or life challenge, I think of Miss Jones as she walked out the front door, shaking her head. Her girls had been provided for, even without her help.

Lord, let me never forget the good things you have done. Thank you that we will always have soup, until Jesus comes! Amen.

More Christlike
ELAINE WRIGHT COLVIN

God, I know you're not in a hurry.
Your plans for me are on time.
You need no schedule or
reminders
For I'm always on your mind.

I know you have drawn the mosaic
And you're fitting each tile in place.
As I continue to follow your plan,
Help me not hurry or race.

Waiting is so often difficult,
And patience I don't easily learn.
But to have my life more Christ-
like
Is what I seek for and yearn.

So as my life's pattern continues
And the next part begins to unfold.
It's you I'm trusting and praising.
It's your hand I cling to and hold.

191

Water-Walkers

DOROTHY SEGOVIA

*In the world ye shall have tribulation: but be of
good cheer; I have overcome the world.*
John 16:33, *KJV*

The passage above is one of the classic
Christian lines. Yet we hesitate to accept it. Tribulation doesn't bring out the cheerleader in us.

Tribulation is a mud puddle we don't want to
splash around in. It feels more like a swamp swallow-
ing us up. But Jesus cautions that we will always be
swamped with storms. Only faith keeps our heads
above water, instead of under the circumstances.

How do we sail the victory vessel and overcome
the world? This calls for water-walking faith. Only
with eyes focused on Jesus can we overcome the
floods of confusion, and get rescued from drowning
in despair.

From a world awash in sorrow, we turn our eyes
the other way, hoping to float over the troubled

waters of our time. If the priesthood of believers is to become the bridge over troubled waters, we must exhibit water-walking faith and so identify with Christ that His passion becomes our passion, His walk becomes our walk.

Oh, Lord, I pray that the wind of your Holy Spirit will fill my sails and guide me to your safe harbor, reminding me that the waves of this life cannot prevail against me. Amen.

Hidden Treasures

JOSEPHINE SMITH

*I will give you the treasures of darkness, riches
stored in secret places, so that you may know
that I am the Lord, the God of Israel, who
summons you by name.* Isaiah 45:3, *NIV*

During the war, candy was scarce. My
sweet tooth was always craving satisfaction. Fruit
was plentiful, but natural sugar just didn't get the job
done.

One Christmas a friend gave me a plate of fudge.
The first bite was delicious. As the day wore on, I had
several more bites. Oh, the sweet satisfaction! I
wanted to devour the entire plate, but I resisted the
temptation and decided to save some for the next day.

When I awoke the next morning, I remembered all
my cousins were coming for dinner that day. Immediately, I thought of my plate of candy. I knew if each of
us had just one piece that plate would be empty by

evening. After much thought, I decided that since it was my gift, I would save it all for myself. I carefully wrapped the dish in a napkin and hid it under my bed. I could almost taste the sweet pleasure I would have over the next few days by saving all of it.

By mid-morning, the families had all arrived. The day was spent in feasting, fun and games. Caught up in the fellowship, I forgot about my hidden treasure. I loved my cousins and enjoyed all the fun we shared.

By late afternoon, my thoughts returned to the plate of sweets under my bed. Several times I was tempted to share the treasure, but my selfish desires won out. Greed became my master.

As the cars were leaving the drive, I ran to my bedroom to uncover my hidden treasure. My taste buds could almost savor the delicious flavor of the fudge. My feet could not run fast enough to carry me to the delicacy. But when I peeked under my bed, my heart sank into my shoes. There was Trixie, my dog, with chocolate all over her face. The candy plate was empty!

That day I learned that hidden treasures are not always the sweetest. How often I have hidden Jesus, the sweetest treasure on earth, from the eyes of someone I love. I hide Him under a bushel of things only to discover that in the end I am the loser.

Lord, help me to share you with all those who cross my path today. Amen.

Three Strikes-
You're Safe!

PAULA MICHELSEN

*As a father has compassion on his children, so
the Lord has compassion on those who fear
him.* Psalm 103:13, *NIV*

Get a hit, Joey! Pick out your pitch!
Have fun!"

From the moment my son picks up a bat to warm
up, his baseball coaches are giving him positive
encouragement.

"You can do it, Son! That's the way to protect the
plate! Good eye, Joey! Good cut, nice swing!"

When I'm not there to cheer him on, I'm across
town supporting my daughter. Her coaches, too,
offer encouragement. "Way to go, Jinny Mae! Show
them how to hit! Yeah, you're a hitter! Way to watch,
Jinny!"

Both my children are fortunate to have coaches who care more about the kids than winning.

There are those games when the other team has a "megaphone mouth" for a coach—cursing and bellowing—who makes more than his team cringe. The kids are scared enough of the bat and ball, petrified by the pitcher, without being harangued by their own coach. Their players' white knuckles and shaky knees remind me of myself when I'm intimidated by a world that hasn't learned yet how to lose.

I'm thankful for coaches like Joey's and Jinny's, who give that ready word of encouragement, that fatherly phrase of support from the dugout. And when the umpire yells, "You're out!" their reassuring word rings across the diamond, "That's OK! You did your best! Good try!"

I wish every parent could hear what I did after one of Joey's games. His coach said, "I had a talk with your son. I told him I'm his friend. I'm out here to help him. If he's got a problem or a question, he knows he can come to me with it. He knows I expect 100 percent, but it's OK to strike out. We're here to have fun and learn. He's going to be just fine."

I walked away from the field, savoring the message. It spoke to me as a word of reassurance from my heavenly Coach. When I can take the "strikes" in life, pick up and go on, then I'm living the way a King's kid can. Then I'm not all tied up in knots of insecurity, intent on my errors and inabilities.

As I sit and watch fly-outs, grounders, foul-tips and strike-outs, I'm relearning important lessons about God and human nature. Thanks to baseball season and a few coaches, I have been reminded of how to "swing and miss" with God. When I'm called

197

"out" in this world, I can hear instead my Father God say, "That's OK! You're still safe at home with me!"

Dear God, thank you for being my Coach. Protect me from discouragement and self-effacement. Keep encouraging me from the dugout, despite my batting average. Amen.

Lord, He Doesn't Know You!

KATHLEEN PARSA

He that believeth on him is not condemned:
but he that believeth not is condemned already.
John 3:18, *KJV*

F red, our dear neighbor, suddenly discovered that he had terminal cancer. His days, perhaps his very hours, were numbered. As a Christian, I had meant to share my faith with him, but had found it difficult, and I continuously put it off. Now I couldn't put it off any longer.

I called the hospital, and the nurse explained that Fred was semi-comatose, but could have visitors. A nurse myself, I knew that normally the last sense a person loses is his sense of hearing. Fred still might hear and understand my message. I prayed all the

199

way to the hospital for wisdom, for our time to be protected and for Fred's heart to be receptive.

He didn't respond when I took his hand or when I wiped the perspiration from his forehead with a moistened cloth. Nevertheless, I explained to him how Jesus loved him and died for his sins and wanted to give him peace and eternal life.

Then I said, "Fred, if you want Jesus to forgive your sins and come into your life, will you squeeze my hand?" Almost instantly, I felt his hand tighten around mine. Although his eyes were still closed and he seemed otherwise unresponsive, he did respond. I then prayed aloud thanking God for forgiving Fred for his past sins and asking God to send His Holy Spirit right now to indwell Fred. I ended with, "Thank you, Lord, that right now Fred belongs to you forever."

As I looked up I noticed tears rolling down from Fred's closed eyes. His hand moved up to his face in an attempt to wipe them away, but in his weakness he missed the mark. With tears in my own eyes, I grabbed a tissue and wiped his eyes for him.

When Fred died two days later, I both rejoiced and wept while praising God for His faithfulness. I thought; *Yes, my intentions have always been good. But, why did I put it off for so long?*

Dear Lord, make me more sensitive to your Holy Spirit's nudging to share you with those who are hurting or lost. For we don't know what tomorrow holds, and our time, indeed, is short. Amen.

For All Mankind

CHERYLL KELLY

And we have seen and do testify that the Father sent the Son to be the Savior of the world. 1 John 4:14, *KJV*

The first time I saw a series of Inuit (Alaskan native) paintings of the Crucifixion, I was deeply moved and humbled by their stark honesty.

In those pictures, the men who condemned Jesus to death wore no tunics or togas, but rather great northland parkas with seal fur lining. Those who mocked our Savior were not misunderstanding Jewish peasantry nor hardened high priests, but rather veterans of the whale hunt, experts with the harpoon. To the bold Inuit artist, the men who nailed the Lord to the cross were not only Roman, but Eskimo as well.

Suddenly, I knew more fully the meaning of

Christ's passion and death. He died for all mankind. Each person's sin, whether Alaskan Indian, African, Chinese or white Anglo-Saxon, made that atoning death necessary. Each of us has a vital stake in the supreme sacrifice—whatever our race, creed or color.

Oh, Lord, let me see with the honesty of the Inuit artist that I, too, helped to crucify you. Help me to live for you. Amen.

My Treasures

ELOISE BUSHA

For where your treasure is, there will your heart be also. Luke 12:34, *KJV*

Tucked away in the corner of a closet is a box containing treasures from my past. About once a year I examine the articles, which represent special events and times in my life. I relive each memory one by one, as I touch each item, and remember.

Here is my father's violin—minus some parts, but, oh, the memories. Memories of my father who died many years ago. Memories of his music as the family gathered around the piano for a music fest.

Here is an autograph book that reminds me of childhood friends and activities. It also contains a poem written just for me by my great-grandfather when he was 93 years old. I remember the family reunion that brought him to our state from his home in Montana, and how excited we were to meet this grand old Civil War hero.

As I rummage through, I find my high school yearbooks, graduation cards and photos that remind me of happy school years. And here I find a wedding book, the bride and groom figures from the top of my wedding cake and the small white Bible I carried to the altar.

Next I find my children's birth identification bracelets. And here are the plaster molds of their handprints, made as Christmas gifts in kindergarten.

Digging a little deeper I discover a group of little plaster wall plaques made by the children in Bible school one summer: "Jesus Loves Me," "God Is Love," "I Am the Light of the World."

Now I find graduation announcements, cards and programs—the closing of yet another chapter in my life, as my children stepped into the adult world.

As I contemplate these treasures, I give thanks to my heavenly Father for all the beautiful memories. But I think now of my most valued treasure of all— the gift of eternal life through Jesus Christ.

I have no mementos of this gift to be put in a box and stored on a shelf. No, this beautiful gift is a part of my life that must be remembered daily, as I share it with others, so that they, too, may have the ultimate treasure of God's eternal love—the best treasure of all!

Heavenly Father, help me daily to realize what a wonderful treasure you have given me. And help me to share this treasure with others. Amen.

The Magenta Colored Blouse

MARY FRANCES FROESE

"I know the plans I have for you," declares the Lord, "plans to prosper you and not to harm you, plans to give you hope and a future."
Jeremiah 29:11, *NIV*

The magenta colored blouse flirted shamelessly with me as I window-shopped. The third time I returned to look at it, I knew it was mine.

I wore my new blouse right out of the dress shop. A peacock never preened with more pleasure than I did that afternoon. The color consultant was right—magenta is my color!

On laundry day a few weeks later, I stood at the ironing board pressing my beautiful blouse. I love to pray while ironing, so I was thanking God for allowing me to have this lovely blouse—and for how special I felt when I wore it—when the phone rang.

After chatting with a friend for several minutes, I

returned to finish the blouse. Placing the iron down on the blouse front, I mmediately heard a sizzle, and the smell of burning fabric assaulted my nostrils. Horrified, I lifted the iron to see a huge, crinkled black hole where the front of my blouse used to be. "Lord! Why did you let me do that to my new blouse . . . you could have stopped me!" I cried, as I sank to the floor—gulping big angry tears and holding tightly to my still smoldering blouse. Finally, I grew quiet and looked at the situation. Sad and frustrating though it was, I wondered: Lord, is there a lesson in all of this?

Immediately, I felt Him whisper to my heart: *It isn't ruined.* Not ruined? I was holding it in my hand and could see it was a hopeless mess! Again: *It isn't ruined. Go to your closet.* Puzzled but obedient to the inner voice of God, I rushed there.

Now what? In looking, I was amazed to see several outfits that the blouse could be worn under, with only the still beautiful sleeves and collar showing. Amazing! The blouse was still good for something.

"Father, what does all this mean?" I exclaimed, convinced by now that I was in the midst of a teaching session. Again, He spoke: *My child, this blouse is just like you. You were once new and very lovely, but you allowed sin to flaw you. I didn't throw you away in my anger; instead, I am using you as an enhancer in my kingdom, for you are very precious to me.*

Father, thank you that you don't give up on your children. Instead, you use our sins and mistakes to teach us of you. Amen.

Never Late Again

NANCY GRAEME DETJEN

You alone are my God; my times are in your hands. Psalm 31:14,15, *TLB*

I was late to everything! Only a little late, a few minutes, perhaps 10 or 15, but late. I knew as God's witness in my mission as a high school principal in a large urban high school, there were those who would consider this a defect in character. How could they see Christ in me if I were always running behind and constantly checking my watch to hurry on to the next appointment?

I had prided myself on an open-door policy; teachers, parents and students felt free to drop by. As they began to share, I would glance at the wall clock, look exaggeratedly at my watch—anything to convey the message that my time was valuable.

But the conferences became longer. When people feel rushed, they zero in on you, look you straight in the eye so you can't look away, and embellish stories with agonizing detail. I would try to cut them off, finish their sentences—anything to free myself. I was desperate. I was always late to my next appointment, and always late for my family.

During devotions the word "times" struck me. I looked in all the translations, and the word was "times," not "time" (as in all eternity). "Times"— plural. What did that mean to me? Then came a revelation! Each piece of time was ordered by Him. I was not to try to control time. He would control it for me. My "times" were in God's hands.

I threw away my clock and gave away my watch. When someone said, "Do you have a minute?" I would not cringe, but say, "Sure, come on in." Then, I would begin to pray silently, "Lord, help me to listen. Help my words to be your words." That silent prayer quieted my spirit and helped me to focus intently on the person across from me, for whom God had ordered this particular "time."

Do you know what happened? The conferences became shorter and I was never late.

I now realize that each piece of time, whether it's listening to others, waiting in traffic or fixing dinner, is ordered and special. Truly my times are in His hands.

Father, Abba, thank you for ordering each piece of time in my life. Only you are in control. Amen.

Treasures to Be Found!

LOUISE B. WYLY

Man looks at the outward appearance, but the Lord looks at the heart. 1 Samuel 16:7, *NIV*

I f I'd seen that dirty old rock, I wouldn't have even picked it up," my friend commented as she looked at my geode, a souvenir from our trip to Colorado. "The outside is dirty and crusty," she said, "but where they've split the rock open, the inside takes my breath away."

As we sat there admiring the inward beauty of this rock formation, we both marveled at the way God had formed crystals within.

Later, I reflected upon her words. My thoughts returned to the day when God had picked me up. No one else would have stooped to pick up this fruitless life. But God saw beyond that dingy crust to the beauty He had placed within.

As I continued to think about this geode, I realized someone had taken the time to break it open so the inner crystals could be visible to the naked eye. This reminded me of how God had to break me. He wanted to teach me to trust Him in every phase of my life. But only after He prepared me, could He proceed to polish me. Only then could those inner crystals be seen by others.

God has a wonderful plan for each person He has chosen. He knew even before He created this world what beauty He would bring forth from our lives. He sees beyond the outer crust to that beauty He has prepared within, and He wants it to shine forth in all the radiance He intended.

Then I wondered: *When I look at others, do I see only the outside?* With God's help, I need to search beyond and look for the potential He has placed within each person. I need to remember that no life is worthless.

Thank you, Lord, for breaking me open and for bringing forth that beauty you have placed within me. Amen.

And the Little Children Shall Lead Me

MARY HARRIS

Jesus said unto her, I am the resurrection, and the life: he that believeth in me, though he were dead, yet shall he live. John 11:25, KJV

My mother's sudden death last October left me reeling with grief. In the midst of mourning, I received a request to teach a class of five-year-olds in Sunday School.

I accepted the assignment, knowing that it was a call from God. He knew what I needed most just then. One of the first lessons, on Easter Sunday, covered the story of Christ's resurrection.

The lesson manual suggested that the teacher tell about death on a personal level, and affirm that we will be resurrected someday if we believe in Christ. I told the class how I had cried when I received word that my mother had died, and that my son, who was then five, had asked why I was crying.

"Because I won't see Grandma anymore," I told him.

"Yes, you will," he replied, "after the resurrection."

When I finished this story, one five-year-old asked incredulously, "Didn't you know that?"

Yes, I knew that. But in my grief over my mother's death I had neglected to believe it, as my class had, without question or hesitation. Their simple, innocent faith reminded me of the words of Mother Teresa: "Never let anything so fill you with sorrow as to make you forget the joy of Christ risen."

That Easter Sunday I learned a lesson. And from that moment, the grief that had engulfed my life began to be lifted.

Heavenly Father, help me to view all of life's disasters as part of the plan of salvation, and grant me your solace in times of sorrow. Amen.

Wrestling Alligators

APRIL HAMELINK

For who has despised the day of small things?
Zechariah 4:10, *NASB*

"Hannah! Sit still!" Trying to fasten tiny white buttons on the back of a pale pink dress worn by a wiggly, impatient two-year-old only added to my sense of total frustration. Anyone who wanted to wrestle alligators should train by trying to dress two preschoolers for Sunday School! Added to my frustration was a husband still in bed, a dress that needed ironing and the smell of burning eggs. What I wasn't preparing was a heart for worship.

Something had to change. I spent the next weeks determined to make Sunday morning a time of harmony. I ironed dresses on Saturday night and got my husband out of bed by waving eggs and toast under

213

his nose. We instituted new rules: no TV on Sunday morning, and breakfast as a family.

All of these changes were wonderful; they smoothed out the mornings. But I realized the most important change had to be in me.

I had perceived the act of worship as something to be done on a certain day of the week, in a certain place, with certain people. How limiting that was!

Now I realize that my worship is also made up of small things like washing clothes and wiping noses, making dinners and taking trips to the zoo. It's telling my children stories about Jesus and praying for my husband's growth and ministry at work.

Worship is an attitude rather than an action. It's the daily celebration of living in Christ.

Father, let my attitude be a celebration to you, and my worship truly pleasing in your sight. Amen.

Hurting—
Who, Me?

GAY LEWIS

*As a father has compassion on his children, so
the Lord has compassion on those who fear
Him.* Psalm 103:13, *NIV*

Once again I greeted a new day with a
vague, empty feeling inside. This had happened several days in a row, and I was puzzled.

I went down the checklist of my heart once more,
looking for a reason for its unsettledness. My relationship with Jesus was special and sweet. I had a
wonderful husband and a good, solid marriage. Our
three grown daughters loved the Lord and their hus-
bands. The fourth daughter, still very young, was a
delight to our middle-age years. My writing was fulfilling. I was blessed with wonderful friends and many

God-fearing relatives. I even had a couple of fantastic little grandchildren. Life was rich and full, with its share of joys as well as problems to solve.

So, what on earth did I have to complain about? I had so much: how could there possibly be an empty place anywhere?

As the morning progressed, the nagging emptiness persisted. Finally, in desperation, I grabbed my Bible and plopped into my favorite chair.

"All right, Lord," I pouted, "show me what this is all about."

Opening my Bible, I turned to a story that had fascinated me lately: John's passionate account of Jesus' crucifixion. I read the familiar words describing the scene at the foot of the cross.

"When Jesus saw his mother there, and the disciple whom he loved standing nearby, he said to his mother, 'Dear woman, here is your son,' and to the disciple, 'Here is your mother'" (John 19:26,27, *NIV*).

I suddenly burst into tears. Longing that had been denied and suppressed for years revealed itself. I heard my voice cry out, "Oh, God, how I've wanted a son! All these years I've longed for a son."

I wept for a long time. Finally, God began to heal the tender wound I hadn't even known was there.

It wasn't that I had wanted boys instead of girls. It wasn't even that I wanted a baby boy to raise. My longing was for that special mother-and-grown-son relationship I'd observed in other families, the same kind of relationship I saw between my husband and our grown daughters.

For years, I'd been denying that desire, telling myself how rich I was, feeling too foolish to acknowledge the pain, when all the time the Lord was ready and waiting to fill and heal my aching heart.

Lord, please make me honest with you. Don't let me forget that you care about each hurt, no matter how small or unworthy I think it is. Amen.

A Stranger in the Tub

MARLENE ASKLAND

*If then God so clothe the grass, . . . how much
more will he clothe you? . . . For . . . your
Father knoweth that ye have need of these
things.* Luke 12:28,30, *KJV*

Driving down the freeway with my husband, I noticed a little man with a packsack almost as big as he was. He walked slowly, as though forcing himself to take each step.

"Honey, stop!" I exclaimed. "That man is in terrible pain."

Stopping, we discovered that he had large holes in the soles of his shoes, causing him excruciating pain. He was grateful for a ride.

We took him to our home, fed him, and talked to him about the Lord. We let him have a bath and offered him a night's lodging.

"I wish we had a pair of shoes for him," I said to

my husband, as the man was bathing. A few minutes later, the phone rang. The wife of one of our parishioners called. Her husband was having chest pains and needed prayer.

"We would come over," my husband explained, "but we have a stranger in the bathtub. I don't want to leave him here alone with the girls. We'll pray from here. Call us if the pain doesn't ease up."

About a half hour later, our parishioner was still in pain. And the stranger was still in the bathtub.

"Honey, you go without me," my husband said. "Let me know how he is."

I went, joining my friends in prayer. The chest pains eased. Then I told them about the stranger.

"I just wish I had a pair of shoes for him. But where am I going to find a pair at midnight?"

The wife's face lit up. "You know, about 12 years ago my grandson left a pair of tennis shoes here, and just the other day I ran across them. I wonder if they'll fit."

"They have to be the right size," I exclaimed. "God knows this man desperately needs a pair of shoes."

Praise God! He not only knows the number of hairs on our heads; He knows the size of our feet!

Thank you, Father, for making provisions for your children. Forgive us when we take them for granted. Amen.

The Best Time of Life

JOY P. GAGE

This is the day which the Lord hath made;
we will rejoice and be glad in it.
Psalm 118:24, *KJV*

Like many mothers, I have a memory box. Labeled "Mother's Treasures," it contains fragments and scraps, childish drawings and notes, hospital menus, pressed flowers and assorted trivia. I have made no attempt to organize the contents. Taken separately, each item is a link to the past, decipherable only by the collector. Lumped together, the collection could be viewed by others simply as a mother's vain attempt to capture time in a box.

Memory boxes are fine in their place, so long as we keep things in perspective. But we should never fall into the trap of living in the past.

I came dangerously close to this after all my children were raised. I longed for the past, when I had experienced the joys of motherhood. In fact, when mothers of young children expressed their frustrations over having no time to themselves, I often told them, "This is the best time of your life."

Then one day a young mother challenged me by replying, "That's what everyone tells me, but no one tells me why."

I had to reconsider what I had said. "Well, it's not the diapers, or the bottles or getting up in the middle of the night," I admitted. Obviously my empty-nest perspective had affected my thinking.

Later, while mulling over this incident, I realized that my young friend and I had similar problems. We were both searching for that magical "best time of life." She was rushing to the future, while I yearned for the past. In the process, neither of us was particularly enjoying the present. In short, we were enduring life instead of enjoying it.

Many mothers are caught in this "other time" trap. When the children are small, mothers look ahead—dreaming of all those tomorrows when there will be fewer responsibilities and more time for themselves. Then comes the day when all the children are gone. Suddenly the mother is longing for all those yesterdays when the children were little. Somewhere between tomorrow and yesterday, today often gets lost.

I still have my memory box, and I often happily anticipate certain future events. But since my encounter with my friend, I have a different outlook on life. When is the best time of life? Life is best enjoyed in the present tense. Whatever time you are in, take each day as a gift from God. Soon you will find you are *enjoying* life, not just enduring it.

Lord, thank you for the gift of life on this new day.
Help me to rejoice in the ordinary, and not be caught
up waiting for the spectacular. Amen.

Let His Light So Shine
DIANTHA AIN

The good is us
is the God in us,
though sometimes
it's hard to see.
It hides
beneath our worldly fears
and our vulnerability.

As we seek it out
in others,
we expose our own
as well.
Then the love of God
lights up the world,
like a shining citadel.

Hearing with God's Ears

DORIS GREIG

Before they call, I will answer; and while they are yet speaking, I will hear. Isaiah 65:24, *KJV*

I was rushing around trying to get dinner ready for my husband and houseguests. Our visitors had flown into Los Angeles from Central and South America and, with no time in between to rest, they were whisked away for a full day of meetings on Christian education principles. I knew they'd all be tired and hungry, so as I prepared their dinner, I prayed that God would give them a special measure of rest. They needed to wake up the next morning refreshed and ready to absorb more information on teaching, in order to go back and enrich the Sunday Schools in their countries.

It had been a hectic day for me, too. Just as I

began last-minute preparations, the doorbell rang. I ran to answer it. A friend had stopped by to drop off a folder of information for my husband.

"How are you, Doris?"

I began to tell her that I was a little tired and frazzled around the edges, when I noticed she wasn't listening. Before I could finish my response, she said, "That's good. It's nice to see you." And with that she left.

I walked slowly back to my kitchen, feeling lonely and deflated. My friend had let me down when I could have used just a word of encouragement, maybe even a quick prayer.

Mechanically, I began to set the table. *Why didn't she hear me? Doesn't she care how I am? I just needed a little of her time.*

And then I heard the words: *Doris, you've done this to people, too. Let this be a lesson to you. Listen to those I send across your path. Give them at least five minutes, even if you are in a hurry. Stop and pray with them.* As I continued to prepare dinner, I had a little talk with Jesus. I asked Him to forgive me for judging another before I looked at my own heart. I confessed my weakness and sin in the same area.

God's promise in Isaiah 65:24 reminded me that He never fails me. He is always there for me, even before I call upon Him. He hears me even when my brothers and sisters in Christ do not.

Dear Lord Jesus, thank you for hearing my silent calls for help. Help me to take the time to hear the heart cries of others. Make me a good listener and encourager. May I hear with your ears today. Amen.

Take Your Foot Off the Brake!

PAULA MEINERS YINGST

Cast your cares on the Lord and he will
sustain you; he will never let the righteous fall.
Psalm 55:22, *NIV*

Careful!" I warned my husband. "Oh,
. . . sorry. It looked like he was coming into your
lane."

From behind the steering wheel, Chuck glanced
over at me with a wry smile, as he maneuvered our
27-foot motor home through Southern California traffic.

"I was watching him," he assured me. Knowing
how nervous I sometimes get when I ride in the front
passenger seat, he added, "You don't have to sit up
here if you don't want to. I'll call you if I need help
again reading the map."

I unbuckled my seat belt and traded positions

with our 10-year-old son, Jonathan, who implicitly trusts his dad and revels in riding up front. Actually, I trust Chuck, too. It's all those other "crazies" on the road that, on occasion, make me dig my fingers into the upholstery and press my foot against an imaginary brake pedal.

I settled onto the padded bench at the rear of the motor home. Though I felt less threatened, the panorama was limited through this narrow side window—not at all like the scene I'd observed beyond the expansive windshield.

I scolded myself for allowing worry to dictate how I viewed the world. Then I realized that I'm often guilty of the same in regard to my spiritual life.

God has faithfully proven to me that He's a highly skilled and capable "driver." He's even promised to protect me from the "crazies" if I obey and trust Him. Why then, do I grab the wheel when He has offered to steer? Why do I allow clawing fingers of fear, doubt, and wrong attitudes to prevent me from enjoying the scenic blessings He offers? And why, pray tell, am I tempted to put on the brake every time he says, "Follow me"?

Father, forgive me when I focus on circumstances instead of on your promises. Help me to trust, and not be afraid. Amen.

Kurokujin

GEORGALYN WILKINSON

He must become greater and greater, and I must become less and less.
John 3:30, *TLB*

Suddenly, the houselights dimmed. Exquisite silk brocade curtains opened, and before my eyes was the lavish set for an afternoon performance of Japan's Kabuki Theater. Many times, as a missionary wife in Tokyo, I was asked to accompany a tourist friend to the famous classical art form, where the folklore of that great nation was magnificently enacted.

The sets were incredibly simple, yet they more than adequately conveyed the drama's location and atmosphere. Costumes were elegant, with colors shimmering across the stage as brilliant as the morning sun. Voices rang out in command or in quiet surrender. At times, shouts from the audience encouraged an actor in his spotlight performance. How easy it was to be lost in the history, the trauma, the agony and joy of life, as depicted by the actors.

Amid the fast-paced drama, I was always fascinated by the quick and subtle changes in costume or landscape. For the actors didn't leave the stage. They were transformed before our eyes—and yet, not exactly. It was the artistic and clever *Kurokujin* who, completely dressed in black, and with black veils covering their faces, entered the stage swiftly and in careful movements to redress a main character. They changed scenery and moved objects, gave swords to the hero or brought a baby for the mother to hold. Sitting in complete darkness, I was never really aware of specifics, only a dark form as it moved in precision on stage. I knew that performance was made even more exciting because of the work of that "unnoticed" performer—the man in black.

I was haunted by these selfless, anonymous, unidentified performances from those never listed on the program or publicly named. How much they added to the total effectiveness. They caused everyone to center on the main characters, the total theme—the reason for it all. Yet their whole obsession was to remain unseen.

In some of my quiet times with the Lord, I've asked Him to let me become like a *Kurokujin*. I pray that I would be so centered on the main character in my life—Jesus—that no one would notice me at all. May my inner being and outer actions turn attention to Him whom I love more than life, and may I always keep Him center stage in my life.

Lord, show me today, by my availability and reactions to life, new ways of causing you to be seen more clearly. Amen.

Panic in the Fog

MARY HAMILTON WEST

When you pass through the water, I will be
with you; and when you pass through the
rivers, they will not sweep over you.
Isaiah 43:2, *NIV*

The tiny island could only be reached at low tide. Even then one had to wade a half mile through knee-deep water. I loved to go there, challenged by the unusual rocks, tidal pools, sea shells and the constant cry of sea gulls overhead.

But at high tide the island disappeared. Its channel waters ran swiftly and the undertow could be strong.

On one occasion I overstayed my island exploration. I hurried to get off while the water remained shallow enough to cross. To my consternation, the water was already up to my waist, and very cold. I leaned against the current and pushed toward the beach.

Then, with a jolt I realized I could no longer see ahead. The shoreline! Where was it? One of the swift and sudden seasonal fogs was rapidly descending upon me, becoming thicker by the moment. Soon a dense wall of fog surrounded me.

My heart began to thud. Panic engulfed me. Which direction should I go? If I chose wrong, I would walk toward open sea. With the deepening tide, I would soon be over my head, unable to tell in which direction to swim. My bearings had vanished and I felt helpless.

"Oh, Lord," I prayed, "I'm totally lost. Help me!"

His still small voice told me to look down—not up or out or around, but down. It dawned on me that if I followed the direction of the waves running toward the mainland's shore, I would end up there, too.

Half walking, half swimming, with the waters up to my chest by now, I began my journey through the fog, keeping my eyes fastened on the wave line. Gradually the water became shallower. After what seemed an eternity, I found myself at last on shore.

I knew that it was God who had directed me to look down toward the wave line. I knew, too, the reality of His promise in Isaiah. He had surely been with me through the waters. He had not let them sweep over me.

Dear Lord, let me ever hear your voice telling me the direction you choose for my life. And, Lord, don't let me wait until I'm in trouble before I start listening! Amen.

Facing Death with a Smile

STEPHANIE VERNON

Even while walking through the dark valley of death I will not be afraid, for you are close beside me, guarding, guiding all the way.
Psalm 23:4, *TLB*

In the mid-1970s, I was trekking through western Nepal in search of Tibetan refugees. It was August—the worst of the monsoon season. My porter had carried medical supplies on his back from India to the Shining Hospital in Pokhra, Nepal, for many years. A retired old man now, he was still strong enough to carry my 60-kilo load of Bibles, records, a small record player and my sleeping bag.

For 17 days, rain had poured steadily. Each day we encountered mountain slides, flooded rivers and roadside bandits. At one point, several bandits with swords jumped out from behind boulders, ready to attack. I dreaded the thought of being struck from behind, so I kept on walking sideways and flashing my best smile. My porter, who was slower than a snail, finally caught up with us. He made a sign to the bandits with the scarf he wore wrapped around his head. That satisfied them and they disappeared between the boulders.

It was a rugged, 17-day trek, full of danger, but rewarding. I found a camp with 3,000 refugees who had never before heard the name of Jesus. Eagerly they received the Bible portions, and attentively listened to the gospel message on records—in their own language.

Later, when I saw the porter again, I asked, "What did you tell the bandits back on the road?"

"I told them that you were not worth killing, because you didn't have anything but books," he replied.

Thank you, Father, for loving and caring for all humanity, and for keeping your messenger safe from harm. Amen.

God's Gentle Reminder

BARBARA LOCKWOOD

Let the words of my mouth, and the meditation of my heart, be acceptable in thy sight, O Lord.
Psalm 19:14, *KJV*

Sunday morning at our house can be the most unpleasant day of the week. One Sunday the alarm clock didn't go off on time; my little son, David, couldn't find his black shoes; I had forgotten to iron my husband's shirt and the eggs burned while I was buttering the toast.

Ten minutes past leaving time, a very angry mom shoved her toddlers into the car, spewing out complaints about our family being late for church again. I wondered why we were even going, as grumpy as we all were.

Shortly after we were on our way, the billowing madness that engulfed my thoughts was interrupted by a voice from the back seat.

233

"Mommy, can you help me learn my verse?" David passed me his paper from last Sunday. "Will you read it to me, please?"

I hesitated as I began to read: "Let the words of my mouth . . . and the meditation . . . of my heart . . . be acceptable in thy sight, O Lord. Psalm 19:14."

"That's too long!" David exclaimed. "I'll never get it before we get to church."

"We've got 15 minutes. Let's do it one part at a time," I answered. Each time I repeated the verse I felt more like a hypocrite. The words stung. This was just the verse that I needed that day. I repeated it dozens of times for him. Each time was more convicting than the last. Constant repetition of His Word had pushed out the bitter, unloving thoughts, and made way for kindness.

Gradually, the sting softened my heart.

"Isn't that just like you, Lord?" I prayed silently. "You pour out yourself in perfect measure, just when we need you most."

Lord, when my words and thoughts are not acceptable to you, gently nudge me. Amen.

Connecting the Dots

LOU ANN SMITH

The Lord will fulfill his purpose for me.
Psalm 138:8, *NIV*

Squeezing a pencil tightly between his fingers, my five-year-old-son Dustin sat at the kitchen table hunched over an activity book. His tongue was pushed out on the left side of his mouth and curled under until it almost touched the side of his chin—a sure sign that this was intense work.

"Whatcha doin'?" I asked, tousling his hair and bending over to see his latest masterpiece.

"Making a picture," he announced proudly. Then he held up a dot-to-dot portrait of something that I could tell was supposed to be Mickey Mouse. Actually, it resembled an unraveled ball of yarn, for he had connected the first dot with the twelfth, and the twelfth with the second.

"Honey, you should draw a line from number one

to number two and then follow each number in order."

"Why, Mommie? he asked.

"Because," I explained, "the person who designed this picture had a purpose for all those black dots. When you join them together in the proper order you'll have a complete picture, just the way the artist planned it."

We turned to a fresh page. I put my hand over Dustin's little fist and gently helped him move his pencil from dot to dot, in the proper order.

As we were finishing the picture of Goofy, I thought about the black dots in my life. Dark blots of trials, mistakes, hurts and unplanned events clutter the landscape of my days. Because I don't see the end results, it can all seem confusing. Rarely have I recognized a pattern or an order of events. So often I want to go from number one to number ten and skip the stops in between!

Thankfully, there is a Savior who gently guides me. What to me is seen as a mystery is really a finished portrait that will someday look just like Him. As the Master Designer, He is fulfilling a purpose in my life by connecting the dots—in the proper order.

When our pencil reached the last number, Dustin squealed, "Oh, Mommie, now I understand!"

I gave him a squeeze.

"So do I, Honey."

Thank you, Lord, for knitting me together and designing the days and events of my life in the way you have purposed. And thank you for gently guiding me when I might otherwise wander around aimlessly. Amen.

Bagels and Swiss Cheese

PAULA MICHELSEN

Three times I pleaded with the Lord . . . But he
said to me, "My grace is sufficient for you, for
my power is made perfect in weakness."
2 Corinthians 12:8,9, NIV

Do you ever feel cheated when you bite into a Swiss cheese sandwich and come up with a mouthful of holes? I do. I wonder why I'm willing to pay full price for a sandwich that's half air. But, then, why do I prefer drinking a can of sugarless, caffeine-free fizz with no nutritive value?

This year it seems I've acquired an unusual taste for nothingness—for emptiness, fatigue and discouragement. From my outward appearance you'd never guess I've felt more like "Swiss cheese" than the usual "sharp cheddar." I've met the deadlines at work, and I've made all the soccer and ballet lessons, and even found time to volunteer for extracurricular actvities at church.

But inside I've often felt like the middle of a bagel—empty. I've just been rolling along, admitting "I can do it!" If I ever felt like a candidate for super-mom, it's not now. Instead, I've learned a lot about humility, like being able to say, "I'm sorry, I blew it!" or "I goofed—I shouldn't have said that!"

At work, with my employees, I've had to repeatedly admit shortcomings. At home, my husband and children know Mom's not perfect. I feel more like a "blow-out" than a "burn-out," since I can't blame hormones—I'm too young to be in a mid-life crisis!

I found myself wanting to quit my job, go on vacation, sleep for days. But these are all unrealistic escapes—or escapades—that wouldn't honor God. No; instead, I want to bring Him glory by getting up every day and taking my family and job seriously, no matter how inadequate I feel.

The whistling wind of the Holy Spirit has found a way to breathe through the nothingness of my human nature. I can see God's strength reaching through my "hole-iness" to touch others around me. I've come to the humilating conclusion that God wants me weak and wobbly, so He can be more visible.

Maybe that's why I've come to savor Swiss cheese this year; I've learned to develop an appetite for the unseen.

Dear God, thank you for making something out of my nothingness. Help me recognize your strength in my weakness. Amen.

Alone or Alive?

CYNTHIA BUCKINGHAM

"For I know the plans that I have for you,"
declares the Lord, "plans for welfare and not
for calamity to give you a future and a hope."
Jeremiah 29:11, *NASB*

As I threw clothes in one box and packed dishes in another, the reality of what was taking place hit me. The divorce my husband had wanted was now part of my life. A cold chill flowed over me.

Weeks later, I sat silently in the living room of my new home, where my three-year-old daughter and I had moved. I thought of what my life would be now that I was alone—a thought that would recur every day.

The door bell rang; he was standing at the door, the father of my child. He had come to take Christy for a visit. As I watched the car drive away, my heart froze. A family that was once together was now broken.

Searching for new direction has been my greatest task. The emotional pain of loss seemed to cloud over any chance for repair. I felt like death was upon me.

But, with a smile and a verse from God's Word, a friend talked to me of the grace and restoration of life. "This is something my father shared with me from the book of Jeremiah," she said, and she read Jeremiah 29:11.

While I did not heal right away, I found a link to rebuilding my soul. I learned that *trust in what God has for my life* brings greater assurance than anything I might find on my own.

What a comfort to know that God protects and loves so unconditionally. What a comfort He is to me.

Dear Lord, on my knees I pray for your loving arms around me. Please comfort my aloneness. Gather me into the center of your peace. Amen.

Unemployed? Oh, No!

MARLENE BAGNULL

He got up, rebuked the wind and said to the waves, "Quiet! Be still!" Then the wind died down and it was completely calm.
Mark 4:39, *NIV*

I knew something was wrong as soon as I picked up the phone.

"I've just lost my job," my husband said.

"Oh, no! Why? What happened?" I tried to control the panic in my voice.

"Financial cutbacks," he said with a sigh. "I'm not the only one who's been let go."

Several days later I went to church for the dress rehearsal of the play I had written for the children's choir. One of my special little friends came running up to me and pressed something into my hand. "It's a gift for you. I got it at a garage sale."

"Oh, it's beautiful, Janeen," I said as I admired

241

the blue sailboat pin. I fastened it to my blouse and gave her a hug.

The rest of the 25 choir members arrived and we began the rehearsal. They were all wound-up, nervous, enthusiastic and very loud as they sang our theme song: "I'm His kid and He's my best friend. He will never let me down . . . . "

I believed those words when I wrote them. *Why*, I asked myself, *can't I believe them now?*

I glanced at the pin Janeen had given me. The sailboat reminded me of that storm on the Sea of Galilee, the terror that had gripped the disciples and the way Jesus calmed the sea.

I kept them afloat, just as I'm going to keep you afloat, I felt the Lord say.

As I write this, three months later, my husband is still out of work. But we haven't gone under. Some days the waves of worry and fear still crash in on me. I wonder if we'll ever again experience smooth sailing. Perhaps not. God never promised us a problem-free life. But He has promised always to be with us. We can know His peace in the midst of life's storms.

Forgive me, Lord, for those times when I have doubted you. Thank you for speaking to me through a child's gift. Amen.

Miracles Do Happen!

DIANE REICHICK

*And all things, whatsoever ye shall ask in
prayer, believing, ye shall receive.*
Matthew 21:22, *KJV*

D r. Murphy walked in and sat down at
his desk. "I'll be frank; the test results aren't good. It
shows the cyst on your right ovary is dark and very
dense. I recommend immediate surgery."

"I'd like a second opinion," I said, as I bit my
lower lip fighting for control.

"Well, you'd better get one fast!" His face flushed,
and he tapped his pen on his desk waiting for my
reply.

"Okay! I guess I don't have a choice." Angry tears
welled up in my eyes.

Then Dr. Murphy explained procedures to me. He
said, "The surgery is similar to a cesarean; you will
have to sign papers for a possible hysterectomy.
Then, you may need chemotherapy."

243

He concluded with, "If that cyst bursts before we remove it, and it's malignant, the cancer cells could consume you." Not at all what I wanted to hear.

I felt numb as I left the medical building. When I pulled into our drive and came to a stop, I smashed my fist into the steering wheel. "Why me, God? Why me?"

The night before my surgery, I paced my hospital room aimlessly. A nurse gave me a sleeping pill, but it had no effect. I walked to the waiting room down the hall and tried to read. Instead I thought of our children, who were then only five and seven.

Finally, I returned to my room, got into bed and sobbed desperately, "God, help me. Please help me." Immediately, I saw an aura of white light surrounding my bed; I felt God's presence around me. Instantly, trust replaced fear, and like a whimpering child cradled in her Father's arms a wave of peace swept over me, and I fell asleep.

The next morning I was wheeled into the operating room, where the anesthesiologist administered the drugs to put me to sleep. Dr. Murphy stroked my arm.

When I awoke, I felt drugged, but no pain. Dr. Murphy walked in, his florid complexion paled, his air of authority crumbling through a cracked voice as he said, "I can't explain it. The cyst disappeared. We didn't have to operate."

I smiled, for I knew a special secret. God had defied medical science in answer to my simple prayer.

Dear God, by my faith in you and in the power of prayer, I believe anything is possible. Amen.

Unbridled Praise

JOAN BAY KLOPE

My feet stand on level ground; in the
great assembly I will praise the Lord.
Psalm 26:12, *NIV*

It is her love of books that prompted me to introduce my two-year-old daughter to the library just a few weeks ago. It was also my desperate need to read something besides *Are You My Mother?* at nap time!

I had heard that our local library gave special attention to the very youngest readers and I was delighted with what I found. But my greatest joy came from Megan's response to the books, puppets, cassette tapes and fish tank, all appropriately placed at her eye level. And although I had explained in the car that the library is a place to be quiet, her enthusiasm could not be contained. With wide eyes she ran to the children's section, squealing and clapping with delight. Thank goodness it was story hour. Her lack of library etiquette merely rounded out the noisy, wiggly assembly of children waiting for the stories to begin.

After reading to the children, the rather unconventional librarian (outfitted in a Hawaiian shirt and high-top tennis shoes) picked up his guitar and explained that it was time to sing a song. Again Megan shrieked with glee, for singing is one of her favorite activities—in Sunday School as well as in the car. The librarian chose a song we knew, "If You're Happy and You Know It." Megan was ready, even though she was instructed to kick her feet during the third verse instead of saying "Amen"—a slight departure from the way she had been taught. *No problem,* I thought. *She will follow the others around her.*

Megan participated in the first two verses with great accuracy. But while dozens of legs kicked to the words of the third verse, I suddenly realized that not only were Megan's little legs working, so was her voice. Ringing clear and strong above the crowd came an unbridled "Amen!"—sung just as she always sings it! My pint-sized evangelist certainly turned heads and prompted smiles. But most of all she showed me what true worship is all about.

Precious Lord, may I never feel ashamed or be afraid to make public my feelings of joy and praise for you. After all, there is so much to be joyful about! Amen.

You Belong to the Family

DAISY HEPBURN

*You are members of God's very own family . . .
and you belong in God's household with every
other Christian.* Ephesians 2:19, *TLB*

The school bus drove up in the muggy afternoon sun to our house in Puerto Rico. Our first grader bounded off the van, calling good-byes to driver and friends in the same breath as he greeted his little sister and me.

We had wondered how he would fit in as he started his education in the bilingual setting of the Mennonite school. Only five, our son had become as comfortable speaking Spanish as English in the first few months of our ministry there.

That day he thrust a bundle of wide-lined papers in my hand, his face beaming with accomplishment. I proudly examined his work; but then I realized: *they were not his papers.*

"David, honey, these are not your papers!" At the top of each page was carefully lettered David *Rodriguez.*

247

"David, you know these must belong to some other boy. You'll have to take them back tomorrow."

"No, Mom, those are mine!" he exclaimed.

"But, David, you know how to print your name. Why did you write it like this?"

"Because I want my name to be Rodriguez. The kids can't say Hepburn; they can say Rodriguez real good!"

How I understood his five-year-old need to belong—to feel accepted—to have others know his name. Sometimes that need keeps me a prisoner in the family of the familiar, unwilling to risk new relationships, new situations, even unfamiliar areas of Christian service.

God tells me in Isaiah 43:1 that He has called me by name, that I am His, that I am precious to Him, honored and that He loves me!

"She Has Her Father's Eyes," is a song that beautifully affirms every Christian's family resemblance. I want to make that my aim each day. I want to carry the family resemblance—and the family name—into all that I say and do. And most important I want to remember that my security lies in the fact that I belong to God's family.

I assured our son that the other children would soon be able to pronounce his name. Then I reminded him how special it is that he bears the name of our family, and of the family of God.

Dear Father, in those moments today when I need to feel the security of belonging to the family, remind me that I am a beloved member of your household. Amen.

Please, Stop the Noise!

ANDREA STEPHENS

Thou wilt keep him in perfect peace, whose mind is stayed on thee: because he trusteth in thee. Isaiah 26:3, *KJV*

The pounding of my neighbor's clanging hammer echoed through the stillness of the early morning. The annoying sound dug into my nerves like the nails being hammered into the wood.

Why did my neighbor have to choose 7:30 A.M. to start making repairs on her deck? After all, this was the only time I was going to have all day to steal a few peaceful moments to sit out on my own deck and read my Bible. *If I weren't a Christian,* I thought, *I'd holler over the fence and ask her if she had to be so inconsiderate.* But my neighbor was not a Christian, and my suggesting that she was impolite was no way to lead her to Christ.

Nevertheless, I was trying to have my quiet time!

Quiet time. Perhaps the idea doesn't require quiet. In fact, perhaps we are being too idealistic in our busy lives to expect the absence of sound during our "quiet times." Could it be that requiring absolute quiet is merely a convenient excuse not to spend quality time in reading and in prayer? Does our devotional time necessarily depend upon the noise level of our surroundings?

For many, the preciousness of actual quiet moments only exist before 5 A.M. and after 11 P.M. Our days are filled with children at play, crying babies, washing machines, buzzing offices, ringing telephones and the chatter of fellow workers.

I discovered that morning that devotional time with the Lord doesn't require quiet *around* me, but quiet *within* me—where it matters the most. I began to ask the Holy Spirit to fill me with His priceless peace. Then I closed my eyes and focused on Jesus. I took a few deep breaths and asked the Lord to calm my thoughts and clear the way for Him to speak to me as I read from His Word. With a quiet heart and mind, I read, prayed and meditated on my favorite Scriptures.

Bang, bang, bang went my neighbor's hammer. Was she still working on that deck? For awhile I hadn't even noticed.

Lord, as I approach my quiet time each day, help me to block out distracting noises and keep my heart at peace, focusing on you alone. Amen.

Adequate to Comfort?

JOY P. GAGE

My strength is made perfect in weakness.
2 Corinthians 12:9, *KJV*

Nothing in life had prepared me for what I saw and felt as I entered the neonatal critical care unit. As I picked my way through people and paraphernalia, I sensed that my presence was an intrusion into this highly technical world. I wanted nothing more than to get out of the way. But a nurse, seeing my confusion, assured me that family was always welcome, and pointed me to the isolette labeled Dustin Jackson.

There, under a plastic wrap tent, his 1-pound, 13-ounce body attached to a maze of wires and tubes, lay our firstborn grandchild. A feeling of utter helplessness seized me. Not only was I powerless to do anything for our grandson, I felt there was very little I could do for our daughter, Carrie, Dustin's mother,

251

who was fighting her own battle for survival.

Her struggle had begun two months earlier, when pregnancy complications sent her to the hospital and kept her there, flat on her back, until she went into premature labor and was flown to this city some 200 miles from her home. While Carrie made a remarkable recovery, her little Dustin survived less than three months.

From the onset of the pregnancy complications and throughout the months Dustin lived, our daughter had been caught up in a hope/despair drama. I, in turn, faced the daily challenge of encouraging and comforting from afar, for we lived over 700 miles from them. I could only "reach out" via the telephone.

Often I hung up the phone feeling overwhelmed by my inadequacy. There was little I could do other than listen, pray with her and, most of all, just let her cry. But letting her cry seemed hardly an adequate response.

Fifteen months after Dustin died, Carrie presented me with a lovely book for Christmas. In it she had written a series of "I remember" messages. One of them read, "I remember you letting me cry whenever I needed to. I remember that you never told me, 'Don't cry.'"

God can use what we consider to be totally inadequate efforts. Even when we are helpless, He is not. Even when we cannot fix everything for our children, God is at work.

God, help me to remember that you are the Great Comforter. Help me to reach out to those who need your comfort, even when I feel totally inadequate. Amen.

The Mud Puddles of Life

MARILOU FLINKMAN

By whom also we have access by faith into this grace wherein we stand, and rejoice in hope of the glory of God. Romans 5:2, *KJV*

W e packed the camping gear and our family of seven children into two cars and headed for a weekend at the ocean. As soon as we arrived, the youngsters ran for the beach, with my cries of, "Don't get wet" echoing in the breeze. My husband and I rolled out the big tent and the array of aluminum poles, and proceeded to put up our temporary home.

As soon as we found a place for the last pole, making the big green and yellow tent look almost secure, the first child returned. Standing with head down and big brown eyes peeking up was Ken. "I stepped in a hole," he said.

I looked at the puddle gathering at his feet and

tried to remember which box held his dry clothes. Mel rigged a clothesline while I toweled off our son and found him a fresh set of clothes. Ken's chagrin touched my heart and I couldn't scold with much conviction. He was cold and wet, and he trusted me to take care of him.

My heavenly Father is like that. He sends me out on the beaches of life with the breeze of time in my face. He tells me not to fall into the puddles of sin, but in my rush to take it all in, I fall in a hole.

When I drag my dripping soul back to Him in faith, I know He will take care of me. His kind touch towels me off and gives me a fresh start.

Dear Lord, thank you for the times you've picked me up, dried me off and sent me out again. Amen.

Baby Talk

KATHLEEN PARSA

*So shall my word be that goeth forth out of my
mouth: it shall not return unto me void, but it
shall accomplish that which I please, and it
shall prosper in the thing whereto I sent it.*
Isaiah 55:11, *KJV*

Like most mothers, I delighted in talking
to my babies. I tried to avoid excessive baby talk,
however. I wanted to say something meaningful. So,
because I believed Isaiah 55:11, I recited Scripture to
my little ones.

Changing diapers was a favorite time for quoting
Bible verses. Sometimes I'd attach a new verse above
the changing table to help me memorize it. I'd be
careful to speak slowly and enunciate each word.
Soon after the babies could speak their first words,
they could also recite John 3:16, Hebrews 11:6 and
the Lord's Prayer.

Because memorizing and reciting come easily to
the very young, especially when put to music, I also
sang to my babies. By the time they were both three,

the children had a simple repertoire of hymns, and Scripture put to music.

Often, they'd unexpectedly initiate singing sessions. How well I remember the smiles in the supermarket when Joy would begin singing, "His Name Is Wonderful, Jesus my Lord." Then there were times when the words would get jumbled, and Michael would sing, "Trust in the world with all your heart." Amusing, yet another teaching opportunity for me.

Even though the children had little understanding then, they were hearing and being comforted by God's Word.

Now they are teenagers, and I no longer recite with them. But I do listen. And it's there. I can hear God's Word coming through. And I believe it will always be there when they need it, because I believe Isaiah 55:11!

Dear Lord, help me to be diligent in teaching young children your Word. As they grow, help me teach them to appropriate your Word in their lives. And please let them see me doing the same. Amen.

Entries from a Real Mother's Journal

MARY HARRIS

And when Rachel saw that she bare Jacob no
children, Rachel envied her sister; and said
unto Jacob, Give me children, or else I die.
Genesis 30:1, *KJV*

M*other's Day, 1977:* How I dread this
day! The Mother's Day program at church is sheer
torture for a woman without children. I was surrounded by glowing mothers and their angelic children.

My arms ache to hold my own baby, but they are
empty. My four stepchildren are terrific, but they call
another woman Mother. I am nobody's mother.

As I leave the chapel, the youth present roses to
the mothers. Someone hands me one out of pity. I
take it anyway.

Mother's Day, 1980: My first real Mother's Day! I never thought this day would come. Gary and I adopted a newborn last September.

My eight-month-old son, George, sits on my lap at church and wets my new dress. He fusses and wriggles so much I can't hear the service. When he spits up on me, I leave the chapel before the end of the program.

I guess I'm really a mother now.

Mother's Day, 1984: George helps his father pick out a corsage of white carnations for me. I'll always remember the sweet, eager look on his face as he runs to me clutching the gold florist box. I'll never forget how empty Mother's Day—and life—were before George.

Mother's Day, 1986: George gives me a clay key chain he made at school. My stepchildren also remember me—Ron and his wife bring their baby to see "Grandma." Penny calls and Randy comes by. Libby, who moved in with us two months ago, gives me flowers.

In the last 10 years, I have mothered four teenagers and one baby—without giving birth to any of them. Once, like Rachel, I despaired of ever being a mother. Now I can't imagine being anything else.

I have been blessed. I am a mother.

Dear Father, please help me to remember to count my blessings. Even when being a mother tries my patience, help me always to appreciate the role of motherhood you have bestowed upon me. Amen.

Fast Food and Living Bread

NIKI ANDERSON

If a brother or sister is naked and destitute of daily food, and one of you says to them, "Depart in peace, be warmed and filled," but you do not give them the things which are needed for the body, what does it profit?
James 2:15,16, *NKJV*

My children and I parked at our favorite fast food restaurant, hardly expecting the drama that followed. As I nibbled on crispy chicken, I noticed a derelict loitering around the restaurant. The man was unkempt, slim and hunched so severely his torso bent parallel to the pavement. My concern prompted a second look. To my surprise, the pitiful man sat down in the middle of the driveway where restaurant patrons swiftly drove in and out.

"Mommy, we better tell that poor man to move," urged my daughter. Agreeing, I quickly laid aside my lunch. At the same time, a minister driving a van painted with the name of a local church hurried to the confused man and coaxed him from the driveway. We watched as the sincere minister handed him a familiar salvation tract—"The Four Spiritual Laws." The old man looked at the literature blankly, tucked it into his pocket and found a less vulnerable spot to sit. *Will he read it later?* I wondered. *Does he even know how to read?*

Suddenly my heart was gripped by a reminder from the book of James. I explained to my children how we are admonished to meet the physical requirements of the needy, such as clothing and food, as well as to make earnest effort to rescue their souls.

"I think we should buy him lunch, kids," I suggested with enthusiasm.

"Let's do it, Mom!" both children confirmed.

People watched curiously as I approached the stranger. Some looked askance as I leaned forward and asked plainly, "Would you like a hamburger and a soft drink?" He showed me 16 cents in his sweaty soiled palm and muttered something about money. I explained that I would pay. His garbled speech was barely understandable, but his brightening face expressed eager acceptance of my offer. His grateful and repeated, "Thank you, thank you," made our simple act of charity an even greater pleasure.

As the children and I finished our meal, I silently thanked God for a balanced witness. We drove away satisfied that the man had received both food for his soul and food for his body.

Lord, help me always to remember the importance of combining acts of love with words of witness. Amen.

Don't Forget the Butterflies, Ruthie

WILMA BROWN GIESSER

*I am the resurrection and the life; he who
believes in Me shall live even if he dies.*
John 11:25, *NASB*

It had been a long night. My sister, Ladonna, was dying, and we who loved her so dearly couldn't stop it. But how we had tried. We had trusted God. We had prayed—I had even fasted and prayed.

We had taken Ladonna to the best cancer specialists and had changed her diet drastically. We cared for her lovingly and tenderly, day and night. We fed her, bathed her, read and sang to her, rubbed her feet and back, and plumped her pillows. We told her jokes and laughed with her—and we hid our eyes so she couldn't see the tears.

Ladonna, too, trusted and prayed. Yet this was to be her final night. She was dying. My other sister, Ruth, held her hand and told her, "Honey, we'll never forget you. We'll see you in every sunrise and in every sunset, in every tree and in every flower."

Looking up at Ruth, Ladonna whispered, ever so softly, "And don't forget the butterflies, Ruthie."

The butterfly—symbol of rebirth and resurrection—what a wonderful reminder! God was freeing Ladonna from pain and heartache. He would resurrect her into a glorious new body, a glorious new life. And she wanted us to remember that.

Oh, God, thank you that someday the heartaches of this world will be left behind. Thanks, too, for the reminder that because I believe in Jesus, I, too, will one day join in your resurrection—in my glorious new body and new life. Amen.

Originally published in *Vital Christianity*, March 6, 1988, published by Warner Press, Inc.

Ordained Praise
(From Psalm 8:1,2 [*NIV*]
ANNETTE PARRISH

Your quasars blink
across 18 billion light years;
a distance that
(written in miles)
would fill my lap with zeroes.

Your signature
is written in everything that lives;
You dot the *i* in "double helix"
and buttercups
change to butterflies.

The rhythm
you clapped out
in one great flash
choreographs the dance
of electrons in a speck of dust.

You bend a light wave
and color
saturates the world;
each bird, cliff, grass, tree
is dipped in its own hue.

You formed me,
and love me
although
I cannot even imagine a color
I've not seen.

And I
play at the seashore
of your universe;
picking up pretty shells,
I hold them to my ear
to hear the ocean.

Meet Our Contributors

LYNN ABBOTT is presently a Masters candidate in the English Education Department at the University of Virginia. She has edited and written for a variety of publications. She enjoys travel, tennis, reading, art and teaching. She resides with her husband, a youth pastor, in Charlottesville.

DIANTHA AIN has won numerous awards for her poetry and music, and has stimulated the writing creativity of over 8,000 school children since 1981. She enjoys piano and theater and writes scores for musicals. She is married, has two grown children and lives in Simi Valley, California.

NIKI ANDERSON teaches home Bible studies, Sunday School and women's groups. She has published magazine articles and devotions. She enjoys cycling, singing, home decorating and nurturing other Christian women. She and her husband reside in Spokane, Washington, with their two children.

DARLENE SYBERT ANDREE has written articles and short stories for Sunday School papers and magazines. She enjoys reading classics and mysteries, canoeing and cross-country skiing. She is married and the mother of three sons. The Andrees make their home in Cinebar, Washington.

MARLENE ASKLAND enjoys calligraphy, painting, reading, gardening and writing stories for children. She and her husband, a pastor, are the parents of four young adults. They live in Woodland, Washington, where they share a Hispanic ministry.

MARLENE BAGNULL is a writing instructor, and founder and director of the Greater Philadelphia Christian Writers Fellowship. Her prayer diary *I Am Special,* for young girls, was published in 1987. She and her husband have three children and reside in Drexel Hill, Pennsylvania.

MARY BECKWITH is a publisher, editor and writer. She conducts workshops on a variety of topics, including writing for publication, and sponsors full-day writers' and women's seminars. She and her husband, Clint, have three grown children and reside in Ventura, California.

MARTHA BOLTON has written six books and has won numerous writing awards. She is a staff writer for comedian Bob Hope, and a 1988 nominee for an Emmy in the category of Outstanding Achievement in Music and Lyrics. She and her husband live in Simi, California, with their three sons.

HILDA J. BORN is presently working on a history of the Mennonites in British Columbia. She has written a variety of articles, and has received prizes for two of her essays. She and her husband of 35 years have five grown children. They reside in Matsqui, British Columbia.

MARGARET BROWNLEY, who teaches writing classes, has six books and numerous magazine articles to her credit. She is a recent winner of the Woman of Achievement award from the National League of American Pen Women. She and her husband have three grown children and live in Simi Valley, California.

CYNTHIA BUCKINGHAM studied with the Institute of Children's Literature. She enjoys sewing, biking and homemaking, as well as writing. A food advisor for her county extension service, she lives with her three-year-old-daughter, Christina, in Redmond, Washington.

ELOISE BUSHA, a writer and music teacher, also teaches Sunday School and conducts workshops on women's topics. She enjoys reading and crafts. The mother of six grown children, she and her husband, Don, make their home in Genesee, Michigan.

MARIAN CARNEY has published a feature article in *Partnership* magazine. She enjoys interior design, hospitality, needlecrafts and travel. Her husband, Glandion, is pastor of Marantha Church in Portland, Oregon. The Carneys have four children.

ELAINE WRIGHT COLVIN directs five Christian writers conferences across the nation and has organized dozens of writers clubs. She has published numerous poems and articles and is listed in *Contemporary Authors*. She and her husband have one daughter. They reside on Bainbridge Island, Washington.

NANCY GRAEME DETJEN is currently a lecturer for California State University in Dominguez Hills. She has worked in the field of education since 1972. Currently on the board for Palos Verdes Community Arts Center, Nancy and her husband have four children and live in Palos Verdes Estates, California.

SHIRLEY DOBSON is an author and homemaker. She has served as leader in Bible Study Fellowship and director of women's ministries for her church, and has appeared on many radio and TV programs with her husband, Dr. James Dobson. The Dobsons have two children and live in Southern California.

DAWN DULAINE currently teaches junior church, and loves working with children of all ages. Her hobby is raising dachshunds. Dawn is married and the mother of two teens. The Dulaines make their home on Bainbridge Island, Washington.

JESSICA C. ERRICO has written for *Aglow* magazine and published her own booklet of Haiku poetry, *Material Musings*. She enjoys painting, reading, singing and Bible study. She and her husband, Anthony, have a daughter and son and reside on Bainbridge Island, Washington.

MARILOU FLINKMAN, who reads at least 100 books a year, is also a busy writer. In addition to being a playwright, she has published 23 articles and short stories in the past year. She is active in her church and local library. Marilou and her husband make their home in Enumclaw, Washington.

MARY FROESE, besides having two articles published, has recently completed a book of family memories. She has coordinated numerous community activities, in addition to being a speaker for Bible studies and retreats. She and her husband have two grown sons and live in Vista, California.

JOY P. GAGE is a speaker, author of several books and has appeared on numerous broadcasts. She is also active in music, teacher training and discipling. She enjoys quilting, swimming, hiking and backpacking. Joy is married, has three grown children and resides in San Rafael, California.

GLORIA GAITHER is a recording artist, singer, lyricist, speaker, teacher and the author of several books and articles. In addition, she was the principal lyricist for more than 350 songs with her husband, Bill Gaither. The Gaithers make their home in Indiana.

WILMA GIESSER is writing a legacy of short stories for her family. For years she wrote technical material related to her employment. She enjoys walking, reading and travel trailering with her husband. The Giessers have three grown children and make their home in Sacramento, California.

DORIS GREIG is the author and founder of the Joy of Living Bible Studies, with over 500 study groups internationally. In addition, she has two other books to her credit. She and her husband, Bill, have four grown children. They live in Ventura, California.

APRIL HAMELINK is a Christian Education major at Seattle Pacific University. She enjoys writing intergenerational Sunday School curriculum, collecting children's books, reading and basket weaving. She and her husband, Pete, have two children and live in Port Orchard, Washington.

BEVERLY HAMILTON has published numerous articles and is writing a book on physical and spiritual fitness. She is a lay counselor for unwed mothers and serves in a personal ministry to her neighbors. Making their home in Fullerton, California, she and her husband have three grown children.

MARY HARRIS is a poet, journalist and fiction writer. She is currently president of the Simi Valley (California) Branch of the National League of American Pen Women. She enjoys needlepoint, reading, quilting and photography. She and her husband live in Simi Valley, and have five children.

PAULA HARTMAN is a travel agent whose hobbies are needlepoint, cross-country skiing and travelling. In addition she is involved in her county's local hospice program. Paula has two daughters and makes her home in Chelsea, Michigan.

ANNA HAYFORD serves on the Council for Women's Ministries at the Church on the Way in Van Nuys, California. She and her husband, Jack, the church's pastor, were recently featured in *Partnership* magazine. Anna enjoys cooking, entertaining, decorating and needlework. Parents of four, the Hayfords reside in Granada Hills, California.

SHERYL HAYSTEAD is a free-lance editor for Sunday School curriculum. She enjoys reading, biking and going to the beach. She and husband, Wes, have two sons and make their home in Ventura, California.

EILEEN HEGEL has published numerous articles and poetry and has her own line of handcrafted cards and calendars. Former co-host for two radio programs for women and families, Eileen enjoys piano and guitar, softball, racquetball and volleyball. She lives in San Diego, California.

BERYL HENNE founded the Christian Writers of British Columbia, which sponsors writing seminars to teach, encourage and fellowship with other writers. She enjoys reading, music and crocheting. She and her husband, Gus, have one daughter and make their home in Delta, British Columbia.

DAISY HEPBURN is the author of five books and eight Bible study booklets. She is a conference and retreat speaker, and founder and director of Hope of Our Heritage women's conferences. She and her husband have two grown children and make their home in San Francisco, California.

MARLA HILL is a Forest Home Women's Auxiliary Bible study leader. She enjoys reading, sewing, singing and teaching God's Word. She is married to songwriter Steve Hill. The Hills have three children and reside in Thousand Oaks, California.

MARILYN HOCHHEISER is a published poet whose

poetry has won several awards. In addition, she has written gospel songs, and the lyrics for a musical. Marilyn and her husband, Sid, have three grown children and make their home in Simi Valley, California.

DARLNE E. HOFFA has written three books, and is a board member for Orange County Christian Writers. She enjoys neighborhood ministries, walking, traveling, reading, entertaining and going to the beach. She and her husband, Jack, have three grown daughters and reside in Brea, California.

BARBARA HYATT is a speaker for Christian Women's Clubs. She enjoys reading and teaching classes on a variety of handcrafts. She is married and the mother of three daughters. The Hyatts make their home in Camarillo, California.

JUDY HYNDMAN has published two articles, and writes children's literature. She enjoys photography, journaling, baking and volunteering at her local library where she has a story hour for children. She and her husband reside in Los Olivos, California, and have two children.

CAROLYN JOHNSON has written several articles and the book *How to Blend a Family*. She enjoys Bible study, church activities and travelling with her husband, Harry. They combined their families to make nine children, all of whom are now grown. The Johnsons live in Solvang, California.

SHARON JOHNSON has published numerous articles and has been honored for the promotion of reading programs in her community. She enjoys camping, hiking, cross-country skiing, painting and snorkeling. She and her husband have four children. They make their home in Issaquah, Washington.

SHIRLEY JOINER is a speaker for retreats and Christian Women's Clubs. She enjoys tennis, skiing and art, and is active in women's ministries. She is a board member for Hope Pregnancy and Adoption Services, and resides in Abbotsford, British Columbia with her husband, Dennis, and their son.

DEBBIE KALMBACH has published in *Virtue* magazine, and is the 1987 winner of the Seattle Pacific University's Christian Writers Conference writing contest. She enjoys piano, swimming and cross-stitch. She and her husband, Randy, have two sons and live in Auburn, Washington.

CHERYLL KELLY has written for *Aglow* magazine and has travelled to international conventions for Women's Aglow Fellowship. She is a soccer mom, Sunday School coordinator and missions committee member. She and her husband have four children and make their home in Everett, Washington.

BERIT KJOS has written a series of Bible studies. Besides writing she enjoys hiking, cross-country skiing and singing. She and her husband, Andy, have three sons. They make their home in Los Altos Hills, California.

JOAN BAY KLOPE is a free-lance writer and editor. She enjoys counted cross-stitch, collecting cookbooks and cooking for friends, teaching, camping, tap dancing, reading and hosting foreign exchange students. She and her husband, Matthew, have two daughters and reside in Ventura, California.

GAY LEWIS has written one book, *Bittersweet,* and several magazine articles. The Lewises have ministered to hundreds of young people in their home. They have four daughters and currently live at and manage a retreat center on the Chesapeake Bay.

BARBARA LOCKWOOD has written three books and several articles. She often speaks on fun ways to present Bible verses, and teaches piano and children's art classes. She enjoys sewing, camping, bicycling and crafts. She and her husband have two sons and live in Brookdale, California.

KAREN BURTON MAINS is well known for her ministry of personal and spiritual renewal. She is the author of several books, a conference speaker, and co-host with her husband, David, of the "Chapel of the Air" radio broadcast. The Mains are the parents of four children.

SHERRI TURNER MARTINELLI is host and producer of "Mother-to-Mother," a weekly radio program in Southern California. She has written articles, advertisements, songs, and a book of poems about first-time motherhood. She and her husband have two children and make their home in Trabuco Canyon, California.

JEANIE MAXWELL has written a bride/baby shower game book and is currently working on *Psalms for Women*. She is a pastor's wife in Oklahoma City, Oklahoma, and mother of two children. She enjoys singing, playing the piano, crafts and teaching women's Bible studies.

RHONDA MCGARRAH has written for various newsletters. She recently chaired the opening of the Ventura County Crisis Pregnancy Center, and now serves on its board. She enjoys snow skiing, camping, walking and tennis. The McGarrahs reside in Ventura, California, and have three children.

MARIA METLOVA-KEARNS is an author, poet and armchair archaeologist. She enjoys teaching Bible classes and studying Hebrew and Greek as they pertain to the Scriptures. She is married to Pastor Albert Kearns. They have one grown son and live in Simi Valley, California.

ZOE B. METZGER writes "many notes and letters," as well as magazine articles. She enjoys sewing, gardening and reading. She teaches Bible classes, and writes skits, plays and devotions for her church. Zoe and her husband, John, reside in Lynden, Washington. They have five children.

PAULA MICHELSEN is a preschool director and has initiated "7-11" clubs for the children in her church. Having completed her first book, she enjoys speaking, and writing plays, dramatic readings and articles. The Michelsens have two children and live in Poulsbo, Washington.

KATHI MILLS teaches classes in writing in addition to being a free-lance writer and editor. Currently completing her second novel, she has had two nonfiction books and numerous articles and poems published. The Mills reside in Santa Paula, California with one son.

SHIRLEY MITCHELL has written three books and published several articles. She writes a column for her area newspaper and has her own radio program. She enjoys travelling, entertaining and horseback riding. She and her husband, Jack, have three children and live in Albertville, Alabama.

LINDA MONTOYA is a writer and speaker who has received numerous awards. She has published in *Guideposts* and *Working Mother*. Linda is active in her church and enjoys leading Bible studies. She and her husband, Frank, have three daughters and make their home in Ventura, California.

LUCILLE MOSES has written articles for her church paper and several special programs. She enjoys reading, ceramics, sewing, crafts, gardening and teaching. She is currently a planner for the Single Parent Fellowship at her church. She has one daughter and lives in Fullerton, California.

GERALDINE NICHOLAS has published numerous articles and poems. A pastor's wife and child care director, she enjoys reading, music and swimming. Geraldine and her husband have three children and make their home in Edmonton, Alberta.

ANNE ORTLUND has written several books in addition to composing more than 250 songs and hymns. She is a partner with her husband, Ray, in a ministry of speaking and writing. The Ortlunds have four children, and live in Newport Beach, California.

GLENDA PALMER has published numerous articles and poems. She enjoys writing song lyrics and greeting cards, and teaching workshops. She is on the board of San Diego Christian Writers Guild. She and her husband, Dick, have two grown sons. The Palmers make their home in El Cajon, California.

ANNETTE PARRISH, a writer and poet, is currently Managing Editor of Youth and Adult Curriculum for Gospel Light Publications in Ventura, California. She enjoys art and American history, breeding orchids, hiking and backpacking. Annette and her husband have three daughters.

KATHLEEN PARSA has had numerous articles published as a free-lance writer for Christian magazines. She is a church leader and Christian activist. She plays guitar, sings and writes music. She and her husband, Dar, have two teens and make their home in Ventura, California.

ALICE PETER has had several magazine articles published. She enjoys American history, travel, learning about the life and customs of Bible times and writing letters to troubled teens. She is the mother of three grown sons and makes her home in Seattle, Washington.

MARGE REARICK has appeared on many television shows with her testimony, and has spoken in churches and women's prisons since 1974. She enjoys art, snow skiing, camping, hiking and playing golf with her family. The Rearicks have two grown daughters and reside in Bothell, Washington.

DIANE REICHICK has published articles and poems in several newspapers and magazines. Besides writing, she enjoys reading, oil painting, calligraphy, restoring furniture, gourmet cooking and gardening. She and her husband, Ron, have two children and live in Simi Valley, California.

JUDITH ROTH has published her poetry in numerous magazines. She enjoys music, art, photography and ministering to young people. She is currently an editorial coordinator for Gospel Light Publications. Parents of one son, the Roths live in Santa Paula, California.

NELLIE SAVICKI is a writer and poet, and is currently editing the Children's Corner for her church paper. Besides writing, she enjoys needlecrafts, dramatics, ships and foreign travel. Just 85, she is "learning to use a computer." Mother of six, she resides in Auburn, Washington.

EDITH SCHAEFFER has authored numerous books. In addition, she and her late husband, Francis A. Schaeffer, founded *L'Abri* (The Shelter) with headquarters in Switzerland. Edith makes her home in Rochester, Minnesota.

ARVELLA SCHULLER is the author of numerous books and a frequent guest speaker. She serves as director for the "Hour of Power" TV program, which is hosted by her husband, Dr. Robert Schuller. Arvella enjoys music and running. The Schullers, who have five grown children, make their home in Southern California.

DOROTHY SEGOVIA, a real estate agent, has published articles in real estate trade publications. She owns Faith Financial Corporation, and is a public speaker, seminar leader and humorist. Dorothy lives with her daughter in Irvine, California.

INGRID SHELTON writes children's curriculum, and also has several books to her credit. In addition she has published numerous stories and articles. She enjoys puppetry, travelling and reading. She and her husband, Philip, have one daughter and make their home in Abbotsford, British Columbia.

ELONA PETERS SIEMSEN is a writer and illustrator. She enjoys song writing, gardening, calligraphy and keeping "normal and exotic" pets. She is the mother of three grown daughters. She and her husband, Armon, reside in Whittier, California.

PAT SIKORA is a free-lance writer, specializing in the areas of health care and inspiration. She is a Bible study leader and author of Bible studies. Pat enjoys reading, travelling, gardening, sewing, cooking and entertaining. She lives in Redwood City, California, with her husband, Bob, and one son.

JOSEPHINE SMITH has published a variety of poetry. She is a retired teacher, bookkeeper and "Jack of all trades." She enjoys art, teaching, speaking and counselling. She is married, has four children and makes her home in Santa Maria, California.

LOU ANN SMITH has written several articles and co-authored the book *Glorious Living*. In addition to being a speaker and soloist for women's retreats, she enjoys playing guitar and piano, and teaching Bible studies. She and her husband, Kirby, have two children. They live in Cameron Park, California.

ELAINE STEDMAN has written *A Woman's Worth*, and has been published in *Decision* magazine. She enjoys gardening, music, birds and being with people. Her husband is Pastor Ray Stedman. The Stedmans are the parents of four and make their home in Palo Alto, California.

ANDREA STEPHENS is the author of *Beautifully Created*, and a second book for teens. She is a local chairperson for the California Junior Miss Program, and enjoys watercolor painting, song writing and playing the guitar. She and her husband live in Solvang, California.

KAY STEWART has written for a variety of publications. She is a member of the Seattle Chapter of the National League of American Pen Women, and has received a Certificate of Merit for Excellence in Children's Music. She and her husband, Don, have five grown children. They live on Bainbridge Island, Washington.

SUSAN F. TITUS is associate director for the Biola University Writers Institute. She has written *Parables for Young Teens,* as well as two leaders guides, curriculum and numerous children's stories. She has two sons and makes her home in Fullerton, California.

DORIS TOPPEN has been published in several newspapers and magazines. She enjoys jogging, gardening, biking, playing volleyball and cooking, and has recently completed a course in lay counseling. She is the mother of four grown children. The Toppens reside in North Bend, Washington.

PATTI TOWNLEY-COVERT has written for and worked in newspapers and advertising for 17 years, and now operates her own typing service. She enjoys reading, crocheting, playing Frisbee, water skiing and going to the beach. She and her husband have two sons and live in Ontario, California.

NEVA B. TRUE has written several devotions and magazine articles, and has completed 12 spiritual journals. She enjoys reading, music and hospitality and ministering to young women. Neva and her husband, who have three grown children, make their home in La Habra, California.

STEPHANIE VERNON is a former missionary, Bible teacher and actress and continues to travel across the United States and world. She enjoys Bible history, maps, oriental food, mountain climbing and foreign languages. She has three grown children and makes her home in San Fernando, California.

CYNTHIA ANN WACHNER has published several articles and devotions. In addition, she teaches a course to writers on how to sell their work. She enjoys gardening, walking, camping, music, cooking and the beach. She is the mother of a son and daughter, and resides in Visalia, California.

LAURIE WARDWELL enjoys reading, cross-stitch, snowmobiling and sharing her gift of hospitality. She has been active on the missionary and women's ministries committees at her church. Currently she is a youth sponsor. She and her husband have two daughters and live in Reedley, California.

ELLEN WEBER is a speaker and Bible study leader. In addition, she teaches classes in writing and has contributed to numerous publications. She enjoys paper tole and reading. She and her daughter, Tanya, make their home in Victoria, British Columbia.

MARY HAMILTON WEST and her husband live in Columbia, Maryland. She teaches Bible studies, speaks frequently at conferences and enjoys needlework, gardening, cooking, music, sports and entertaining. Her husband pastors a church in nearby Catonsville. The Wests have four grown children.

JEAN WESTLAKE is a television co-host in Kansas City, Missouri. A conference speaker and teacher, she also has a counseling ministry at her church. She enjoys cooking, decorating, music writing and reading. The Westlakes have four grown children and live in Lee's Summit.

GEORGALYN WILKINSON is executive director for GLINT (Gospel Literature International). She served for many years as a missionary to Japan, and has also been a correspondent for the Foreign Press Association. Georgalyn, who has two daughters, makes her home in Southern California.

LOUISE B. WYLY has several publications to her credit, both in books and magazines. She is a Sunday School teacher and leads home Bible studies. Louise enjoys reading, china painting, knitting and crocheting. She and her husband have four grown children. They live in Minneapolis, Minnesota.

PAULA MEINERS YINGST has written numerous articles and teaches creative communication and writing workshops. Besides writing, she enjoys volunteering at her children's schools. Paula and her husband, Chuck, have two children and make their home in Vista, California.

Postscript

If you've enjoyed this book, if one of the
devotions has touched you in a special way or if you
have questions concerning your relationship to God,
we invite you to write to us. Address your
correspondence to:

Women's Devotional
Regal Books
2300 Knoll Drive
Ventura, CA 93003.

May God richly bless you!

More Regal Books Written Especially for Today's Busy Woman. . .

A Moment a Day—Mary Beckwith and Kathi Mills
Dale Evan Rogers, Ruth Graham, Shirley Dobson and many other Christian women have written practical devotions that speak directly to women's lives. Each of the over 100 devotions begins with Scripture and concludes with a special prayer. 5419516

Faith and Savvy Too! The Christian Woman's Guide to Money—Judith Briles
A practical guide to money management for women. Topics include how to make money work in today's market, how to use credit wisely, how to make financial decisions and much more. 5419383

**We Didn't Know They Were Angels:
Hospitality Even When It's Inconvenient**—Doris W. Greig
Hospitality is a gift to others that should be nurtured. You don't need sterling silver or a gourmet kitchen; all you need is a willing spirit and an open door. Includes over 300 family tested recipes. 5419750

**Free to Be God's Woman: Building a
Solid Foundation for a Healthy Self-Image**—Janet Congo
A book for the Christian woman who seeks a better understanding of herself and her relationships with those she loves. 5419407

**I'd Speak Out on the Issues
If I Only Knew What to Say**—Jane Chastain
This book explains, in a step-by-step format, what you can do to make your opinion heard. The most hotly contested issues of our day are covered including school-based health clinics, abortion, pornography and more. 5418968

Romancing Your Marriage—H. Norman Wright
Maintaining intimacy and romance in your marriage is possible and fun! Best-selling author Norm Wright shows spouses the benefits from learning to love your imperfect partner, ridding yourself of resentment and trying creative romantic suggestions. 5419168

Look for these and other exciting Regal titles at your regular Christian bookstore!

Introducing the
Joy of Living Bible Study Series

Specially designed for individual, family or small group use. Each book encourages insight into the Word of God. Includes conveniently three-hole punched and perforated pages for personal notebook use.

Exercising a Balanced Faith—Doris W. Greig
This thought-provoking 8-week study focuses on James. it is only when we discipline our lives and give it all to God that we can escape the bondage of worldly pursuits and meet the needs of the world in the way that God desires.   5419649

Discovering God's Power—Doris W. Greig
In this 9-week study of Genesis 1-17 you will find that God's power isn't some intimidating force, it is a power that is available to any believer—when we surrender our will to God.   5419764

Walking in God's Way—Ruth Bathauer and Doris W. Greig
A 7-week Joy of Living Bible Study in Ruth and Esther. These Old Testament books center on God's love and His special compassion for us. They also show how unlikely circumstances will never stand in the way of God's perfect plan for our lives.   5419474

Power for Positive Living—Doris W. Greig
An 8-week Joy of Living Bible Study in Philippians and Colossians that focuses on the Christian life of joy and hope through Jesus Christ. We can be joyful, even in a world of sorrow, if we will stand fast in the knowledge of our Savior.   5419493

Living in the Light—Doris W. Greig
A 6-week Joy of Living Bible Study in 1,2,3 John and Jude. These books focus on the fundamentals of Christianity, the assurance of God's salvation and warnings of heretical teachings.   5419501

Courage to Conquer—Doris W. Greig
This 6-week Joy of Living Study is an in-depth look at Daniel, a companion of kings and a man devoted to his God. Christians can learn many lessons from his uncompromising example. Will we answer the call to go against all odds to reveal our Christian values?   5419489

Look for these and other exciting Regal titles at your regular Christian bookstore!

#301